"This book provides essential and .... our moral obligation to confront s............ ......antle racist structures. Fr. Daniel Horan ....u to prayerful reflection and dedicated action to ad.... ... the God-given dignity of all people."

Jennifer Mason McAward
Director of the Klau Center for Civil and Human Rights
University of Notre Dame

"Important, urgent, and necessary, Daniel Horan's new book challenges all Catholics to face up to the essential challenge of racism in our Church and in society. One of the most promising young theologians working today, he offers a grounded and unflinching look at what all recent popes have called a sin and invites us to become true allies with our Black brothers and sisters in the fight for justice."

Rev. James Martin, S.J.

"This book is a shrewd and urgent guide to a big problem: racism in America's white Catholic Church. Daniel Horan's groundbreaking wisdom both challenges and inspires. Written with wit, charm, and love, this book offers us a vital pastoral roadmap to healing and hope."

Patrick Saint-Jean, S.J.
Author of The Spiritual Work of Racial Justice

"A great book that is sorely needed today! Fr. Daniel Horan offers this insightful, honest, and self-reflective work to help white people recognize that eradicating racism is up to us. This book calls for action and roots that call in the Church's teaching on racism. Every Catholic needs this book and every parish should consider a small-group study of it!"

Rev. Matthew S. O'Donnell
Pastor of Saint Columbanus Catholic Church
Chicago, Illinois

"Daniel Horan undertakes the much-needed and Herculean task of writing about the sin of racism, its effects on white people, and what white Catholics can do about it. This book may be an uncomfortable read, as it will prick consciences and perhaps even anger some, but you should read it with an open mind and heart anyway. Horan does the heavy lifting by answering common objections about the existence of racism and why it is systemic in the United States."

Gloria Purvis
Catholic speaker, podcaster, and radio and television commentator

"Racism is a white-person problem and white Catholics are complicit. But what do we do with this realization? How are we to act? Fr. Daniel P. Horan offers invaluable guidance and resources for white Catholics who hope to recognize and respond in faith to the anti-Black racism in ourselves, in our society, and within our Church. Read this book and study it on your own or in a small group and you will learn a great deal."

Matthew J. Cressler
Author of Authentically Black and Truly Catholic

A White Catholic's Guide to Racism and Privilege

A White Catholic's Guide to Racism and Privilege

Daniel P. Horan

Maryknoll, New York 10545

Founded in 1970, Orbis Books endeavors to publish works that enlighten the mind, nourish the spirit, and challenge the conscience. The publishing arm of the Maryknoll Fathers and Brothers, Orbis seeks to explore the global dimensions of the Christian faith and mission, to invite dialogue with diverse cultures and religious traditions, and to serve the cause of reconciliation and peace. The books published reflect the views of their authors and do not represent the official position of the Maryknoll Society. To learn more about Maryknoll and Orbis Books, please visit our website at www.orbisbooks.com.

Copyright © 2021, 2025 by Daniel P. Horan

Published by Orbis Books, Box 302, Maryknoll, NY 10545-0302.

All rights reserved.

Original edition published in 2021 by Ave Maria Press.

No part of this publication may be reproduced or transmitted in any form or by any means, electronic or mechanical, including photocopying, recording, or any information storage or retrieval system, without prior permission in writing from the publisher.

Queries regarding rights and permissions should be addressed to: Orbis Books, P.O. Box 302, Maryknoll, NY 10545-0302.

Manufactured in the United States of America

Library of Congress Cataloging-in-Publication Data

Names: Horan, Daniel P., author.
Title: A white Catholic's guide to racism and white privilege / Daniel P. Horan, O.F.M.
Description: Maryknoll, NY : Orbis Books, [2025] | Includes bibliographical references.
Identifiers: LCCN 2024037443 (print) | LCCN 2024037444 (ebook) | ISBN 9781626986084 (trade paperback) | ISBN 9798888660638 (epub)
Subjects: LCSH: Racism—Religious aspects—Catholic Church. | Race relations--Religious aspects--Catholic Church. | Racism--United States. | Privilege (Social psychology)—United States.
Classification: LCC BX1795.R33 H67 2025 (print) | LCC BX1795.R33 (ebook) | DDC 241/.675—dc23/eng/20240906
LC record available at https://lccn.loc.gov/2024037443
LC ebook record available at https://lccn.loc.gov/2024037444

"White people have a very, very serious problem, and they should start thinking about what they can do about it."

— *Toni Morrison*

Contents

Preface to the Orbis Edition IX

Introduction XV
    Why This Book?. XIX
    Why Me? XXI
    Why Now? XXIV
    A Note about Language, Style, and Audience XXIX

1. **What Is Racism and How Do We Talk about It?** . . . 1
    Racism Is an Actual Conspiracy 2
    What Is Racism? 4
    There Is No Such Thing as "Reverse Racism" 13
    Further Reading 21

2. **What Does It Mean to Be White?** 23
    Whiteness as a Social Construct 30
    Whiteness as Normative 36
    Whiteness as Property 45
    White Fragility and Rage 52
    Further Reading 59

3. **Racism Is a White Problem** 61
    Why Doesn't Anything Seem to Change? 64
    The Role of White Power 70
    Popular Culture, Media, Society 76
    Socialization and Implicit Bias 81
    Further Reading 86

4. **Systems, Structures, and Institutions** 88
   What America Is and Is Not 92
   Racial Profiling and Police Brutality 99
   Mass Incarceration 107
   Racism and the Catholic Church 112
   Further Reading 124

5. **What Does the Catholic Church Teach about Racism?** 127
   Vatican II and Papal Teaching 129
   Global Perspectives 139
   Statements from the United States Conference of
      Catholic Bishops 147
   Proposals for Anti-Racist Church Leadership 161
   Further Reading 169

6. **How to Be More of an Ally and Less of a Problem** 171
   Recognize the Significance of Your Social Location 174
   Relearn What You Thought You Knew 179
   Develop a Spirituality of Ongoing Conversion 187
   Further Reading 191

7. **Where Do We Go from Here?** 193
   At the Personal and Family Level 196
   At the Local Level 201
   At the National Level 207
   The Urgent Call of Now 210

Acknowledgments 213

Preface to the Orbis Edition

I am writing this preface to the Orbis Books edition of *A White Catholic's Guide to Racism and Privilege* during the same week that marks the tenth anniversary of the killing of Michael Brown, an unarmed Black teenager, by a white police officer named Darren Wilson in Ferguson, Missouri. Brown's death on August 9, 2014, set off a firestorm of righteous indignation and protest, beginning in the streets of Ferguson but eventually reaching cities across the United States. On November 24, 2015, officials held a press conference during which they announced that a grand jury had decided not to indict Wilson, which led to protests erupting in over 170 cities. Protesters chanted the now famous slogan "Hands up, don't shoot," and the sequence of more Black deaths at the hand of police—Brown's in Ferguson and Eric Garner a month earlier in New York—led to the transformation of a 2013 online posting about "Black Lives Matter" by activists Alicia Garza, Patrisse Cullors, and Opal Tometi from an internet hashtag to a real-life movement.

Half a decade later, in the midst of a terrifying global pandemic, another instance of a white police officer killing a Black man would set off a summer of protest on behalf of racial justice and police reform across America, this time under the unifying banner of "Black Lives Matter." The brutal murder of George Floyd by Minnesota police officer Derek Chauvin, which was captured on video by a courageous witness and shared with the world, unleashed a force demanding racial justice and police reform on a scale that the United States had not experienced since the civil rights movement of the 1960s. As you will read in the introduction, this book was born within the context of that moment in history.

The original publisher of this book approached me in the summer of 2020 at the height of the Black Lives Matter protests and public anguish over the persistence of systemic racism and white supremacy in this country. The acquiring editor who reached out to me and encouraged me to consider writing this book was enthusiastic about my manuscript, and other members of the company showed similar excitement about the book.

Nevertheless, I was prepared for the possible backlash such a book might generate. This publisher was best known for books on spirituality, devotional materials, and resources for primary and secondary Catholic education. They had never published something that addressed so pressing a social and ecclesial issue, nor were they prepared for the racist attacks that they were warned in advance (by me and others) they were likely to experience from many of their predominantly white and politically conservative readers.

I had multiple conversations with editors, marketing team members, and other specialists at the publishing house ahead of the book's publication, sharing with them insights from the years of firsthand experience I gained writing, lecturing, and teaching about racism and white supremacy. This was an admittedly volatile subject matter, and there would be many people who would feel uncomfortable at best and others who would be enraged and defensive. In this internet and social-media age, even those who had no previous relationship with the press or its publications could still be swept up in online campaigns of hate and intimidation. The issue was not whether such attacks would be forthcoming but, instead, was the publishing staff prepared to respond to them? Some attacks might merit acknowledgment, while others were best ignored, but a plan and a sense of mission and courage would be required of everyone moving forward. Before the book was published, I received universal affirmation from everyone at the publishing house I spoke with that they were ready and supportive. They were convicted by what the events of 2020 unveiled and understood that a resource like this was (in their opinion at the time) desperately needed in parishes and schools. They were behind the project 100 percent.

And then the book came out, and everything I had warned about came to pass.

I soon learned about external and internal pressures on the house to disavow and stop publishing the book they had asked me to write. I saw online advertising for the book suddenly cease and standard promotion for the book vanished virtually overnight. Nevertheless, I was assured that the house remained proud of the book and would continue to make sure it was available.

And then, two years later and without warning, I received a brief letter from an editorial staffer at the press informing me that the publisher had decided to take the book out of print and, as was contractually stipulated, all the publication rights would immediately revert back to me. I could see if another publisher was interested in releasing the book, but from that point onward the original press was done with it. Although the written justification given was vague and avoided any direct mention of the internal and external pressure campaign to drop the book because of the topic of anti-racism, the rationale for this sudden and dramatic action was clear; the writing had been on the wall for some time.

Despite what I believe were sincere intentions and good-faith efforts by the press and its staff before the publication of the book to address the sin of racism and the persistence of white supremacy within a Catholic context, the ultimate actions speak for themselves: they were not able to withstand the racist interests and attacks of those who denied the reality of racial injustice in our church and society.

I share this unfortunate and disappointing backstory for two reasons. First, it illustrates that the work of anti-racism is difficult and demanding. The press that originally published this book had little previous experience publishing theological or pastoral books that took seriously questions that stand at the intersection of faith and action on behalf of justice. The events of 2020 had inspired many of these same people to examine their hearts and minds, and that examination of conscience led to a sincere desire to do something different. But it is one thing to *want* to make a change, to take a stand on behalf of social justice informed by one's Catholic faith, and another thing to *actually do it* and *accept the consequences* that come with efforts to stand in solidarity with those who suffer from systemic injustices and surrender the privileges and comfort that are standard for those who benefit from the same structural inequities. The short history of this book's publication and its subsequent disavowal by the publisher is a further reminder to people of good will, especially white folks in a white supremacist society such as ours, that there is a cost to doing what is right. This ought to be no surprise to Christians who worship a God incarnate who was executed simply for preaching and modeling a way of living that prioritized the downtrodden, the abused, the marginalized, and the forgotten. Why should disciples of Jesus Christ be surprised that there would be consequences, negative pushback, and even vitriolic attacks for doing exactly what he had done?

Second, I want to express gratitude to Orbis Books and its publisher Robert Ellsberg for their affirmation of this volume and commitment to publish this book within twenty-four hours of the notification from its original publisher that it was cutting ties. The prompt and enthusiastic response to add this volume to the Orbis catalog was a clear affirmation of the impact this book has had already in its first years of publication and a corporate desire to make sure this book continues to be a resource for individuals and communities looking to work toward racial justice and to do so from a position of Catholic faith. Those familiar with the hundreds of books Orbis has published over the years on themes related to liberation theology, racial justice, peacemaking, and nonviolence, among others, will not be surprised to see this book take its place alongside those other important works of political and pastoral theology. Orbis is no stranger to the costs of authentic discipleship (to channel the witness and legacy of Dietrich Bonhoeffer), and therefore it is the perfect publisher for this modest contribution to the work for peace and racial justice. If the idea for this book had been solely mine and not the result of a request from the original publisher, then I have no doubt that it would have been published by Orbis from the start. I am glad it has found its appropriate and supportive home.

In the five years since this book was first published so much has changed and yet far too much remains the same. While the global COVID-19 pandemic has effectively ended, the pandemic of systemic racism in our world and faith communities continues to rage on. White supremacy infects our society, institutions, and churches, which requires white folks of good will to work hard to see the often-hidden dynamics of systemic racism and fight for racial equality by embracing a spirit of ongoing conversion and commitment to faith-informed social justice. I hope that this book might continue to provide an occasion for learning and conversation, serving as a starting point for some individuals and communities to address systemic racism and white supremacy and serve as a refresher and support for those who are further along in this journey. As the story of this book itself reminds us, it is a costly journey, one that requires white folks like me to surrender certain social and ecclesial comforts while seeking to announce the reign of God through word and deed. There is more work to do, but we don't do it alone.

Daniel P. Horan
August 2024

Introduction

I am a white man in the United States. My experience in the context of this nation has been directly shaped by my racial identity throughout my entire life, whether I have been conscious of this reality or not. In fact, my whiteness—or, more accurately, that our society classifies me as something called "white"—has not always been the direct object of my awareness. For most of my life I rarely thought about myself as participating in something called "race," instead viewing people of color as the only ones inhabiting "race" and viewing bigoted individuals (usually white) who spoke racial slurs and overtly discriminated against minoritized communities as "racists." As someone who didn't fit either of those descriptions, I didn't think much about the concepts of race, racism, and racial justice, nor was I really exposed to the reality of their existence in what could be described as my elite and sheltered education. And I know I'm not alone.

The concept of race, perhaps more so than the stereotypical subjects of religion and politics that are not to be discussed in so-called polite company, almost never came up in my household or in the classrooms in which I studied. Sure, my teachers and textbooks presented unthreatening lessons about the progress of the civil rights movement of the 1960s, but there was little that was shocking or inspiring or challenging about what we learned. This complex and significant moment in our past—like the shameful history of chattel slavery and the Jim Crow era—was simply presented as another stop on the timeline of American progress, an opportunity to pause and reflect on "how far we've come as a society" and to figuratively pat ourselves on the back for how tolerant and inclusive the United States is today. But such presentations, while well meaning, were nevertheless untruthful. Not only was the reality of the past *whitewashed* such that it could be presented as a noncontroversial lesson to a classroom of predominantly white children at a private school in Upstate New York, but the manner in which race was discussed also reinforced a sanitized and oversimplified version of a reality that failed to convey the complexity of racial injustice and white supremacy in our country. Classrooms, like gatherings of family and friends and coworkers, were often treated as a form of "polite company" in which such truth telling was implicitly forbidden. Only many years later would I come to realize that the very same dynamic that perpetuates systemic racism, which harms and disadvantages people of color for generations on end, was also a form of structural injustice that covered over such painful realities for white people, effectively shielding them—shielding *me*—from seeing the world as it actually is and from understanding more clearly how I and people who look like me fit into and benefit from it.

In addition to identifying as a white man in the United States, I can also add some other important qualifiers, including that I am a Roman Catholic—born, baptized, and raised—and, more specifically, I am a Franciscan friar, ordained priest, and professor of theology at a Catholic seminary and graduate school. This part of my identity is important too because my faith is one of the most influential aspects of my life and personal history. I went to Catholic schools my entire life, from kindergarten through graduate school, and was raised in a family that took our Catholic faith seriously; we never missed

Mass on the weekend, even when camping in the Adirondack Mountains during summer vacations. My Catholic faith has not only shaped my relationship to God and informed my Christian imagination, but it has also molded my worldview about what discipleship looks like in the modern world, how the Gospel of Jesus Christ calls us to be proclaimers of the reign of God, and how our baptismal vocation includes a universal call to holiness.

As important as my faith tradition has been and remains, the Church that I love and have dedicated my life to serving has nevertheless failed me and countless others at times when it comes to addressing racism. I don't recall ever hearing a homily or religious-education teacher talk about racism, racial justice, or white supremacy in any meaningful or memorable way. My home parish is the largest in a midsize city, one that nurtured my vocation to religious life and priesthood, but one that also knew little racial or ethnic diversity. Most of the people who worshipped in my parish looked like me or my brothers or my parents or my grandparents, all of whom are white. There were a few families of color—a couple families of African descent, a few Latinx families, one family of Indigenous people—but their presence rarely registered in the sea of white faces in a parish that considered diversity largely in terms of whether one was of Irish or Italian heritage. Thinking back now with the clarity of hindsight, I realize that the fact of race was always operative and touched the lives of every person in that congregation. It was just that we were by and large protected from seeing our embeddedness in the dynamics of racism due to the unearned benefits of white privilege that shielded us from that truth. Perhaps some willfully overlooked their complicity in unjust structures—small and large—in order not to face the uncomfortable facts of life.

Many Church leaders did not address racism in homilies, faith-formation programs, or public actions because their own whiteness did not make it easy to "see" what was otherwise plain to people of color. Other Church leaders, recognizing that the issue was more complicated than simplistic popular narratives suggested, nevertheless refused to name the reality of racial injustice—both the fact of racism and the fact of white privilege, the two sides of one coin—because to do so required risking their own vulnerability and putting their disproportionately white congregants in an uncomfortable position.

I recall one instance some years ago when a diocesan priest friend of mine asked for my advice in advance of the weekend liturgies after nationwide coverage of the shooting of yet another unarmed Black man in another state. News coverage of the shooting and the protests that followed dominated the headlines for days. Though he was at first inclined to do so, he was nervous about including a prayer intention for victims of police brutality in the upcoming Sunday liturgy's Prayers of the Faithful. He feared upsetting the largely white congregation, being perceived and accused of "being political," and offending the local police, whom he served as a part-time chaplain. He asked what I thought about including a prayer for the repose of the murder victim and an invocation for reforms to prevent similar violence in the future while also including another prayer for the safety of police as a preemptive form of placation of his would-be critics. I was clear: I did not think this was a matter meriting a "both-sides" response, which is how he framed the proposed compromise. While I have nothing against prayers for first responders and public-safety officials, who have admittedly difficult jobs, this moment called for something else. As people of faith, those who dare to call ourselves "Christian" as followers of Christ—himself an innocent man of color executed by state authorities in his time—we have a responsibility to be bold and direct in our prayer and in our preaching. People would inevitably be upset, because the truth is upsetting. I didn't think it was right to shy away from that uncomfortable truth or to let fear of white discomfort shape our prayer. He took my feedback into advisement. But in the end he decided to scrap both intercessory prayers, preferring not to acknowledge the police murder of an innocent man at all rather than rock the boat of his white congregation's comfort.

This example is one of the least egregious instances of the Church's ongoing complicity in the perpetuation of racial injustice in the United States. My priest friend was scared and nervous, unsure of how to proceed, and uncertain about how to navigate the pushback he surely would have received had he merely taken the simple step of speaking the name of a murder victim in the form of a prayer of lament and requiem. He was at least aware on some level that he ought to say or do something, but in the end his fear won out and he prioritized the comfort of his white congregation over racial justice. If this kind of behavior is going to change, then white Catholics—lay, ordained, and religious—must unlearn the false narratives that we unwittingly appropriated over a lifetime of education in a culture that promotes whiteness as the standard and ideal; and we must relearn the truth of racism and white privilege that we have shielded ourselves from but that is always already operating in our communities and in our churches.

Why This Book?

This book was conceived as a resource for Catholics—white Catholics in particular—to begin the work of relearning what racism in the US context is actually all about. This includes addressing hard realities that white people have typically been able to avoid directly confronting due to the blissful ignorance afforded us by an unjust system of racism in the United States and in the Church. This book is not intended to be a definitive or exhaustive study on racism, racial justice, or white privilege. In this sense, the indefinite article of this book's title—the "A" in *A White Catholic's Guide to Racism and Privilege*—does a lot of heavy lifting and is intended to reflect the aim of this project with sincerity. It is one of many introductory texts geared toward those who are seeking an accessible resource that will not shy away from uncomfortable truths, harsh realities, and challenging questions. For many white people, this may be the first time you have been asked to take a hard look at yourself, your community, your experience, your presuppositions, your prejudices, and your faith through the lens of racial justice. It will be unnerving at times and unsettling to be sure, but the discomfort you feel as a white person confronting the facts of racism in the American context in general and the Catholic Church in particular pales in comparison to the daily risks, threats, and burdens unjustly placed on the shoulders of women and men of color.

This book is necessary because there are so few resources out there aimed at a general audience on this topic, written from a Catholic perspective, and from that of a white Catholic in particular. There are dozens of outstanding books already in print that have helped me over the years come to understand what my sisters and brothers of color have been saying for more than four centuries but that I was unwilling to recognize or unable at first to see. I am indebted to these insightful texts, especially those written by authors of color, and I will reference and recommend many of them throughout this book. There is also a bibliography at the end of each chapter, which provides a thematic reading list for further study and engagement.

As I have indicated already, the primary audience for this book is white Catholics like me, though I also hope that Catholics and other people of color who pick up this book will find its contents affirming and supportive of an effort to promote anti-racism in our communities and churches. I do not pretend to know the first thing about what it is like to be a woman or man of color in the United States. But I do know a lot about what it is like to be a white person in a society and church that is affected by the realities of racism and white privilege, and I know how hard it is for those on the privileged side to accept the truth of complicity in anti-Black racism as well as the ongoing, intentional, and challenging work of becoming a better anti-racist ally. This book is intended to help guide white people to discover those things that we were socialized to not see, to dismiss, to excuse, to qualify, to rationalize, or to reject outright. It focuses primarily, though not exclusively, on anti-Black racism, given the predominance of this discrimination in the United States, but much of what is discussed can also apply to other people of color in many circumstances. This book is intended to be a beginning and an invitation to go deeper in embracing the work toward racial justice in our communities as a constitutive part of what it means to be a Catholic Christian in the United States.

Why Me?

Over the last decade I have found myself convicted by the realities of racial injustice and confronted with my own complicity, privilege, and insulation from seeing reality as it actually exists. It is not easy for me to pinpoint a definitive moment or experience in which I realized there was more to the reality of racism than I had been led to believe (or unconsciously wanted to believe), as if there were a singular instance that hit my psyche and conscience like the flip of a light switch. Some white people have such experiences, but I am not one of them. For me it has been a gradual awakening to the dynamics of the two-sided coin of anti-Black racial injustice and white supremacy.

Over time I came to realize that the God who loves each and every person and creature in the world into existence also calls us to live among one another in a particular way. That way of living, proclaimed by the Old Testament prophets and described in the parables and preaching of Jesus Christ in the gospels, looks very different from the way we *actually live* in the world. We can do better. *I can do better.* I have come to understand that learning about how we live in the world and how God is calling us to do better demands of me more than just doing the personal, albeit important, work of educating myself about racism and white privilege. For me, it means not only *speaking about* racial injustice but also *speaking to* my fellow white people.

I wrote this book because each and every one of us white folks shares the responsibility to work for racial justice and to overcome the pervasiveness of white supremacy in our society and faith communities. Not all of us are called to do the same thing, but each of us is called *to do something.* I am a professor and a priest. My work is primarily in the classroom and in the sanctuary, teaching and preaching, sanctifying and healing in the name of Christ. As an author, columnist, professor, and speaker who has been invited to lecture around the country and throughout the world, I have a distinctive voice and platform from which to speak. And so I must use my voice and platform for promoting the justice, peace, and integrity of creation that God demands from each of us as people of faith. As the Second Vatican Council has taught us, "The Church always has the duty of scrutinizing the signs of the times and of interpreting them in the light of the Gospel."[1] As a member of the Church it is incumbent on me to recognize that one of the most urgent signs of our times is the persistence of systemic racism.

The philosopher George Yancy, a leading expert on race and racism, addressed white people in the preface to the second edition of his powerful study *Black Bodies, White Gazes*. His invitation is direct and discomfiting, which is precisely the point. And the challenge he poses—representative of a larger invitation to people like me who have long enjoyed the blissful ignorance a white supremacist society affords despite the atrocities experienced on a daily basis by people of color—is one that motivates me in writing this book.

> If you are white, though, know that you are part of a system that would rather you live a lie than risk you seeing the truth. If you are white, you *must* face a certain kind of death—the death of your narrowness of vision, the death of your white narcissism, the death of your "innocence," the death of your neoliberal assumptions, the death of the metanarrative of meritocracy, the death of all of those things that underwrite your white gaze as the only way of seeing the world.[2]

This is the challenge before those who, like me, occupy a social location of privilege in a culture that does not merely harm

---

[1]. Second Vatican Council, *Gaudium et Spes*, 1965, no. 4, http://www.vatican.va/archive/hist_councils/ii_vatican_council/documents/vat-ii_const_19651207_gaudium-et-spes_en.html.

[2]. George Yancy, *Black Bodies, White Gazes: The Continuing Significance of Race in America* (Lanham, MD: Rowman & Littlefield, 2017), xxii–xxiii.

certain populations of minoritized people but advantages folks like me and reinforces false narratives about merit, deservedness, and entitlement. And for Catholics in particular, this invitation to "face a certain kind of death" echoes the message of Jesus Christ in Luke's gospel: "Then he said to them all, 'If any want to become my followers, let them deny themselves and take up their cross daily and follow me'" (9:23). Compared to the injustice and harm imposed daily on our sisters and brothers of color over centuries, the cross we white people must take up in the quest for racial justice is, as Jesus says elsewhere, a relatively easy yoke and a light burden (see Mt 11:30).

It is not the responsibility of people of color to "educate" white people. The responsibility is our own. There are plenty of resources available, first-person narratives of the consequences that systemic racism has wrought on individuals and whole communities, scholarly studies and sociological analyses of the indisputable discrepancies that exist as a result of such unjust structures and institutions, impassioned pleas for societal change and ecclesial conversion, that are all readily accessible—that is, if white people have "eyes to see and ears to hear" the unsettling truth (Mt 13:9–16). It is incumbent on white people to educate and challenge each other, to speak the uncomfortable truth in loving but direct words. This is why I wrote this book.

Why Now?

The origins of this particular book can be traced back to the horrifying and tragic murder of a defenseless Black man named George Floyd at the knee of a white Minneapolis police officer on May 25, 2020. A video capturing the eight minutes and forty-six seconds during which Derek Chauvin knelt on the neck of Floyd as the life left his incapacitated body went viral and sparked a national and international response unseen since at least the Ferguson, Missouri, protests in the wake of the police killing of Michael Brown in 2014. But in truth, the size and scope of the protests that lasted for weeks during the summer of 2020 had few precedents, even in the civil rights era of 1960s America. As numerous commentators have noted, the protests in the wake of Floyd's murder included a multiracial coalition and international response unrivaled in the American collective awareness of the ubiquity and deplorability of systemic racism and racial injustice in the United States. Something was different this time. It was not the killing of an unarmed Black man or the deployment of police brutality against persons of color that was novel. Disturbingly, such heinous acts of anti-Black animus, terror, and violence have been happening in the United States since before there was an actual country bearing that name. The difference this time seemed to be the way in which the recorded evidence of the overt violence of racial injustice broke through the societal noise and white denial of the complex structural problem of racism.

This national and global reckoning with systemic racism and police brutality held up a mirror to white America and forced those who had otherwise comfortably avoided facing these facts before to grapple with our social and cultural realities rather than believe the self-referential and self-aggrandizing myths we tell ourselves about American exceptionalism. For many white Americans this was the first time in a long time (if ever) that the shield of white privilege was penetrated by the troubling truth that children, women, and men of color in this country experience the world very differently than the way white people in similar geographic and social locations typically do. The stark injustice, the plain unfairness, the inexplicability of what was captured on film and witnessed by white people—but what has already long been known and feared by people of color—was now more than most decent white people could tolerate. So, why now? On the one hand, I have no idea. Police body cameras and bystander smartphone videos have, for years now, captured similar atrocities in the act. On the other hand, I believe it was simply the last straw. The scale of (white) public opinion had irrevocably tilted, and tilted toward justice in a manner leading to cries of righteous anger in solidarity with those who have been continually harmed by systemic racism.

Many white people have taken advantage of the moment by seeking resources to help them make sense of what they are now only beginning to see with new eyes. Publishers, too, have collectively awakened to the need for resources, especially for those written by authors of color. In addition to supporting and justly compensating writers of color, which I fully support and which was one of the conditions of my agreeing to take on this project, there is also a need for white authors like me to step up and take responsibility for our part in the dynamics of systemic racism that implicate all of us. Part of that responsibility is speaking out and using what social capital and platforms one has to help educate white folks about what we would otherwise prefer to ignore.

So when my editor reached out to invite me to write this book, I had some serious thinking to do. More than a year earlier I had written a more pointed deconstruction of the American bishops' 2018 document on racism.[3] Prior to that I had delivered occasional lectures on racism and white privilege at academic and public conferences, at universities, and in various dioceses around the United States and abroad. As a columnist,

---

3. Daniel P. Horan, "The Bishops' Letter Fails to Recognize That Racism Is a White Problem," *National Catholic Reporter*, February 20, 2019.

I had written multiple pieces on topics related to racism and white privilege. But I had not yet dedicated any book-length effort to the subject.

Part of my answer to the question "Why now?" is to confess that I no longer feel that my periodic anti-racist work is sufficient—and perhaps it never was. While I may have been more aware of the concurrent reality of racial injustice and white privilege in this country and in our Church for a lot longer than many of my fellow whites, the events of the historic year 2020 have fueled a flame of righteous indignation and thirst for justice in me that I cannot ignore. This feeling reminds me of a powerful letter that the American Trappist monk and spiritual writer Thomas Merton wrote to Dorothy Day, the cofounder of the Catholic Worker movement, on August 23, 1961. Feeling his own sense of divine justice stirring in his heart, particularly as he weighed the inadequacy of the Church's response to the devastating signs of his times—the Cold War, nuclear weapons, the civil rights movement, the Vietnam War, and so on—he felt that he had to shift his focus as a writer and a public figure. He explained to his friend and fellow Catholic,

> This, Dorothy, is sometimes a very great problem to me. Because I feel obligated to take very seriously what is going on, and to say whatever my conscience seems to dictate, provided of course it is not contrary to the faith and to the teaching authority of the Church. . . . I also know that somehow God always makes it possible for me to say what seems to be necessary, and hence there is no question that I am completely in His hands and where I am and that I should therefore continue as I am doing. But why this awful silence and apathy on the part of Catholics, clergy, hierarchy, lay people on this

terrible issue on which the very continued existence of the human race depends? . . . As for writing: I don't feel that I can in conscience, at a time like this, go on writing just about things like meditation, though that has its point. I cannot just bury my head in a lot of rather tiny and secondary monastic studies either. I think I have to face the big issues, the life-and-death issues: and this is what everyone is afraid of.[4]

What Merton is grappling with here echoes in many ways my own experience. I also feel as though I can no longer continue just working on theological monographs and books about spirituality, though they have their place. I also feel the pull of conscience and experience the Spirit of God moving in my heart, calling me to take responsibility and speak from my own experience. Like Merton, I am also concerned about the teaching of the Church, which is why this book is aimed at fellow white Catholics. I want to make clear that, though there also exists in our own time "awful silence and apathy on the part of Catholics, clergy, hierarchy, lay people" on the issues of racism and white privilege, this does not mean that people of faith and the Catholic tradition do not have something to say and do in response. It means, quite frankly, that too many people of faith—especially white people like me—have not fully engaged the Catholic tradition and done what is ours to do. This book is intended to help encourage and empower the reader to begin to do something, even if that simply means changing the way one sees the world.

---

4. Thomas Merton, "Letter to Dorothy Day (August 23, 1961)," in *The Hidden Ground of Love: Letters*, ed. William H. Shannon (New York: Farrar, Straus and Giroux, 1985), 139–40.

Why now? Because, as the Second Letter to the Corinthians proclaims, "See, now is the acceptable time; see, now is the day of salvation!" (6:2). There is no other time than the present, and the present demands something of white folks like me because God demanded it first.

A Note about Language, Style, and Audience

Before moving ahead to get into the topics at hand, it is necessary for me to say a few things about the language, style, and audience for this book.

First of all, language is never static. The words we use and the terms we invoke shift and develop over time. Such is the case with how race is identified in the English language. In the wake of Jim Crow–era segregation, it was commonplace for people of African descent in the United States to be referred to, especially by white people, as "colored," a moniker that with the passage of time has been abandoned and is now rejected by most African Americans as offensive.[5] Alternatively, the term "Negro" was understood as a more appropriate and respectful term to reference women and men of African descent. This is why one finds the term used not only by white authors and speakers in the early to mid-twentieth century but also by Black women and men themselves, such as one finds in the writings of Martin

---

5. It is important to note that some Black individuals and communities also used the moniker "colored" in earlier times. Such is the case with the civil rights organization NAACP, which is an acronym for National Association for the Advancement of Colored People. Founded in 1909 by people of African descent and some white allies, the organization has retained its acronym for its title, but no longer publicly uses the full originating name because of the pejorative nature of the descriptor "colored."

Luther King Jr. or James Baldwin. Near the end of the 1960s a number of other terms became more commonplace, arising from within the Black community to refer to those of African descent. This is when terms such as "Afro-American," "African American," and, most importantly, "Black" became increasingly normative. Today, with a growing appreciation for the cultural diversity within the community of African descent in the United States, including those of Afro-Caribbean and other heritages of origin, the term "Black" has become normative, and it is the term I will primarily use throughout this book.

Relatedly, I will sometimes use the phrase "people of color" to describe collectively those who do not identify or are not identified as white. Previously, such groups were referred to frequently in the American context as "minorities," but the shift demographically in the United States toward growing populations of non-whites has rendered that identity increasingly untenable. Furthermore, it is a term that places those who are not identified as white in a subordinate category, whereas "people of color" is an identity that originated in the Black community in the 1960s and has been appropriated by other communities in recent decades.[6] It is important to note that not all non-white people embrace this terminology for collective identity, because it can appear to "flatten" or "homogenize" all non-white persons into some generic category.[7] However, because the phrase arose from within the Black community and is widely embraced today

---

[6.] See Efrén Pérez, "'People of Color' Are Protesting. Here's What You Need to Know about This New Identity," *Washington Post*, July 2, 2020, https://www.washingtonpost.com/politics/2020/07/02/people-color-are-protesting-heres-what-you-need-know-about-this-new-identity/.

[7.] See E. Tammy Kim, "The Perils of 'People of Color,'" *New Yorker*, July 29, 2020, https://www.newyorker.com/news/annals-of-activism/the-perils-of-people-of-color.

by members of other non-white communities, I will regularly use this term along with the relatively new acronym "BIPOC," which stands for "Black, Indigenous, and people of color," at various points throughout this book.[8]

I will refer to those who identify or are identified as Caucasian, white, of European descent, and the like as "white." I recognize the problems inherent in descriptors that can be perceived as binary, but this is the nomenclature used by a majority of Black and white scholars and anti-racist activists alike, and by many if not most white people when they talk about race. This is the terminology I will use in the pages that follow. I have also made a deliberate choice in how I capitalize certain terms referring generally to a racialized population or to a whole group of people, choosing to capitalize "Black" and not "white" throughout this book.[9] When I have directly

---

[8] For more, see Sandra E. Garcia, "Where Did BIPOC Come From?" *New York Times*, June 17, 2020, https://www.nytimes.com/article/what-is-bipoc.html.

[9] The choice to capitalize "B" (Black) or "W" (White) in reference to racialized groups is still a live debate among publishers and editors of periodicals. The trend is moving toward a journalistic consensus that recognizes the difference between an adjectival descriptor ("a black business," "a predominantly white neighborhood") and a pronoun used to refer to groups of actual human beings ("Black people," "White people," etc.). I have chosen to be consistent with the capitalization of racialized nouns throughout this book that refer to people of color. I have adopted the position of philosopher Shannon Sullivan, who explains: "I will capitalize 'Black' when discussing people of the African diaspora and use 'black' simply to indicate color. I will use lower case 'white' for white people since they have not (yet) really figured out a racial identity apart from white supremacy and white privilege, and for that reason, capitalizing 'White' would be misleading and/or confusing for my purposes here" (Shannon Sullivan, *White Privilege* [Cambridge, UK: Polity Press, 2019], 1). For more on the journalistic debate, see

quoted somebody else, I will leave their selected terminology as it originally appeared to maintain the integrity of the citation.

Racism and privilege are tremendously nuanced and complex topics. There is no way in one book to adequately address all the various dimensions, implications, and related subjects that surface when we begin to engage such important, sensitive, and intricate subjects. Therefore, it is important that I state from the outset that the primary scope of this book is limited to anti-Black racism and white privilege in the United States. While there are other communities that can be the object of racialized oppression and even certain minoritized communities that benefit from the stratified system of racial injustice in this country,[10] the long-standing history of relentless anti-Black racism and the continued disproportionate harm inflicted on Black people in this country demands our attention in a distinctive way. I will occasionally make reference to the racial injustice perpetrated against Latinx, Asian, Indigenous, and other communities of color, but I have elected to focus primarily on anti-Black racism given its central place in the American context, including the Church. Likewise, when talking about privilege I narrow my focus to those who identify or are perceived as white in this context.

The style of this book is meant to be informative and well researched but also accessible and direct. Although I am an academic theologian by training and profession, I am also a Franciscan friar who is deeply committed to popular preaching (in both liturgical and other contexts) as well as continuing education

---

John Eligon, "Are African-Americans 'Black' or 'black'?" *New York Times*, June 26, 2020, https://www.nytimes.com/2020/06/26/us/black-african-american-style-debate.html.

[10.] See Michael Omi and Howard Winant, *Racial Formation in the United States*, 3rd ed. (London: Routledge, 2015).

for all people. In the spirit of both accessibility and directness, I have decided to write this book with a deliberate conversational feel. In other words, I am not merely speaking in the abstract or as an "objective" narrator, but instead wish for this book to be a dialogue between me and you, the reader, as well as between us and the authors I am engaging in the pages that follow.

This style arises from the primary audience for this book. While I am not *only* talking to white people like me, I am *principally* directing my thoughts and words to this group. There will be times when I simply use the second-person pronoun "you," and when I do so, I'm talking to "you fellow white Catholics." There will also be times when I use the first-person plural pronouns "we" or "us" or "our," at which point I'm speaking to those who share a similar social location to me—again, other white Catholics. The aim here is not, in any way, to be exclusive or dismissive of people in other racial, social, or ecclesial locations. I actually wholeheartedly welcome anyone and everyone who is interested in unpacking the complexity of and implications arising from racial injustice and white privilege to read this book. It's just that given the vast number of resources already available (many of which are included in the bibliography at the end of each of the chapters of this book) and the narrow scope necessary for this one book, my primary focus will be addressing white Catholics in the context of the United States.

It is also worth noting the refreshingly direct words of the antiracist writer Ijeoma Oluo about the minefield of white people talking about race: "You're going to screw this up. You're going to screw this up royally. More than once."[11] One of the many, many challenges to addressing the persistent reality of racial

---

11. Ijeoma Oluo, *So You Want to Talk about Race* (New York: Seal Press, 2019), 45.

injustice in this country and in our Church is that many whites are too frightened to say *anything* at all about racism or white privilege out of fear of saying the wrong thing or inadvertently saying something offensive or ignorant. So, in the spirit of Oluo's helpful naming of the proverbial elephant in the room, let us just agree that you (just like me) will inevitably make mistakes, say the wrong thing, feel defensive or exhausted at times, and generally be confused. That is absolutely normal and okay, provided that we are sincerely committed to learning from such mistakes and missteps, rather than using those instances as a form of self-justified indignation and cause for abandoning the important work that still needs to be done. Part of the unavoidable discomfort that I have been mentioning includes the recurring realization that what we have thought, believed, said, and done in the past (and perhaps also in the present, and quite likely in the future too) arose from and reinforced structures of racism and white supremacy.

Do not let the discomfort of the truth discourage you from the necessary work and responsibility you and I and all white people must do. When we encounter an idea or fact that tempts us to react in a defensive posture, we must stop ourselves. We must sit with it. We must ask ourselves why we are feeling this way. We must consider what presuppositions we were operating with that led us to feel that this new realization was somehow threatening our sense of self or perception of the world. We must process what it means that this new information or perspective is true, has always been true, but that we had been unable or unwilling to see its veracity before. We must take into consideration what it means that, as a white person in the United States, this information or perspective initially made us uncomfortable, but this same reality may have contributed to a lifetime of oppression, discrimination, dismissal, rejection, and threat to life for people of color.

I wrote this book not because I am some expert here to lecture you about what's wrong with you and what's right with me—far from it. This book is only possible because for much of my adult life I have been grappling with a growing awareness of the insidious nature of systemic racism and its twin evil of white privilege, considering my own inextricable role in that twofold context in which I exist, and exploring the fact that the very mechanism of America's white supremacist culture has hidden these truths from my consciousness from the beginning. While I have learned a lot and studied the dynamics of racism and whiteness more than some people, including many of my brother priests and bishops, there is no "graduation" point for a white person, no definitive moment when any of us can claim to be "racism-free." I am still learning and have a lot more to learn. I have screwed up and I am still screwing up, and I know that I have unintentionally hurt friends, colleagues, and strangers by my racist assumptions or unconscious biases over the years. Sadly, for many such instances, I was never aware enough to realize the harm done in the moment, but there are some examples that I can recognize after the fact, thanks to what I have learned from others along the way, and I will share some of these throughout this book. Like the very core of the Christian vocation, striving to become more and more an anti-racist as a white person in the United States is a lifelong journey of conversion that requires an immense amount of humility and patience. It also requires courage and a commitment to action when called upon to put into practice the anti-racist principles you learn along the way.

1

What Is Racism and How Do We Talk about It?

There are few things more incendiary than to call another person a racist. The reason that many people, especially white people, react so strongly to being labeled a "racist" is that there is a general understanding that whatever the term means, it is not a good thing. In fact, it signals something very, very bad and refers to someone who is, likewise, very, very bad. The moral judgment contained in the term immediately elicits a defensive posture from the accused. Often, the self-defense mechanism that white women and men have been socialized to deploy in such a setting goes into overdrive and, rationally or not, the person accused of being a "racist" (or saying something racist, or doing something racist, and so on) goes into full-on relativizing and dismissing mode in order to demonstrate just how "not racist" they are: *Racist? How can I be racist? I have Black friends. I have a Black spouse. I have Black children. I voted for President Obama, twice! I have never said the n-word. I listen to hip-hop.* And so it goes.

That none of those things, true as they may be in some cases, can inoculate someone from the profound depth and reach of racism—in a society that was built on a foundation of white supremacy and subjugation of anyone not considered "white"—

is lost in the moment as self-conscious white people try to save face. One of the greatest barriers to legitimate, honest, and direct conversations about race, racism, and racial justice in the United States is the defensiveness of those who identify as or are perceived to be "white." The complexity and nuance of terms like "racist" or "racism" are rarely ever engaged because the invocation of those terms tends to send whites into a self-defensive mode that frequently shuts down conversation and prevents any real learning or dialogue. To put it simply, most white people know that to be called a "racist" or to be somehow tied to this thing called "racism" is just about the worst thing one can be accused of in American society. The moral weight of these terms is the only thing that seems to register: racists are bad; therefore, to be called a racist is to be called a *bad person*.

But the truth is that racism is far more complex and insidious than most people realize. If we are going to have any hope of addressing the deep-seated problem of racism in the United States and in the Church, then white people in particular have to willingly risk the vulnerability necessary to learn, to be challenged, and to rethink what they had taken for granted previously. White people in general, and white Catholics in particular, have to accept that they will be made uncomfortable by the reality of racism when they open themselves to the truth that the very structure of racial injustice has prevented them from seeing.

Racism Is an Actual Conspiracy

I am generally not a fan of conspiracy theories, because most of what is presented under such a heading turns out to be crackpot absurdity peddled under the guise of secret truth. But the fact is that some conspiracies do actually exist, and racial injustice in the United States context is a prime example. A real conspiracy involves *conspirators*, individuals and groups and organizations that work together to accomplish a self-serving end. It is a conspiracy to maintain a certain order, power, privilege, protection, and influence for one population while simultaneously denying all of that and more to another population. Unfortunately for well-meaning white folks, the conspiracy is designed not only to harm people of color but also to be hidden from the consciousness of white people. Black people, Indigenous people, and other people of color have known *forever* the truth of this conspiracy we call racism because they have been the victims of it from the very beginning of European colonization of the Indigenous lands we now call "The Americas." Some collaborators in the conspiracy have been overt and clear about their agenda of dehumanization, of genocide, of white superiority, of cultural Eurocentrism, and of land acquisition and wealth accumulation at the expense of the humanity, lives, safety, and future of whole populations of other human beings. But many whites—especially throughout the twentieth and twenty-first centuries—have remained willfully ignorant about the persistence of the conspiracy. When we unconsciously choose to *not know*, we white people are complicit with racism and remain, to borrow a legal term, "unindicted co-*conspirators*." Just because you do not identify with or in any way support explicit hate groups like the KKK or neo-Nazi organizations does not mean that you are free from responsibility. On the contrary, as we Catholics know well from the Confiteor prayer at the opening of Sunday Mass, we are always responsible for both "what we have done *and what we have failed to do."*

This book is an invitation for white Catholics to take responsibility for what we have done and for what we have failed to do as it relates to racism and white privilege. The process and the conversations around these topics will inevitably make you uncomfortable—there is absolutely no way around that, so it's important that you realize this from the outset. I beg you not to shy away, indulge the temptation to become defensive, or dismiss or rationalize things that may seem new or scary or unsettling to you. As Catholic Christians, it is our baptismal duty to live the Gospel and follow in the footprints of Jesus Christ. The model for how we are meant to live in the world is one that always has one eye on the injustices before us that Christ and the Old Testament prophets who preceded him decried in the name of God, while keeping another eye on the likely risk, challenge, and rejection that comes with embracing God's will and proclaiming the reign of God. This is not a call to masochism or self-hatred, but a reminder of our vocation to embrace the truth of the world around us and recognize the unjust suffering that afflicts so many. What will be discussed in this book are hard truths, but the fact that they are difficult and challenging does not undermine their veracity. As people of faith, we are meant to face the truth head-on and respond to it in a manner in keeping with the message of the one who is the Truth, and the Life, and the Way (see John 14:6).

What Is Racism?

Most white people have been taught to understand "racism" in a very narrow way, as a term referring to "bad people." This restricted definition of racism limits the term to description of discrete, particular, and individual *actions*, manifested either in derogatory language or slurs (such as the use of the n-word or invocation of pejorative stereotypes) or in concrete actions (such as the burning of a cross or the physical harm done to people of color). This understanding of what constitutes racism is what Catholic priest and theologian Bryan Massingale calls "commonsense racism." He explains that this limited definition usually describes the following kinds of circumstances:

> Person A (usually, but not always, white) consciously, deliberately, and intentionally does something negative to Person B (usually, but not always, black or Latino) because of the color of his or her skin.[1]

This conception of racism is "commonsense" in that the factors behind the harm done, and by whom and to whom, are as plain as day. On the one hand, there is no disputing that what Massingale describes here is a form of racism. All it takes to recognize it is for someone to have a little common sense. Yet, on the other hand, the narrowly defined circumstances, behaviors, and actions that most white people consider "racist" do not adequately encompass the deep, ever-present, persistent systems of racial injustice and white privilege that are the social ground and foundation for such individual acts. Massingale points out that while we all can agree on the reality of such particular instances of racism made manifest, there are many problems with such a circumscribed definition of a far more complicated reality. This is why I have described racism as an actual conspiracy: because it is a dynamic that involves many different people working in tandem, whether conscious of the dynamics or not, to perpetuate a system that at bare minimum advantages some and disadvantages others.

For example, this "commonsense" notion of racism might alternatively be described as the "a few bad apples" approach. It

---

[1.] Bryan N. Massingale, *Racial Justice and the Catholic Church* (Maryknoll, NY: Orbis Books, 2010), 13.

suggests that aberrant individuals act out in isolated, particular instances in a manner that is overtly sinful and criminal, motivated as they are in their choice of words and actions by a personal hatred of people of color. While there are undoubtedly such people, this "few bad apples" approach masks over the fact that racism is far more than particular acts of racially motivated animus. As Massingale says, "A focus on individual behaviors and attitudes does not adequately explain the existence of a racialized society, where race is a principal lens for social interpretation and understanding."[2] The hard truth identified here is that what most white people think of in terms of "commonsense racism" is but the most public, blatant, and easily recognizable *symptom* of a reality that is much more pervasive and that this book is intended to help identify and unpack.

To say that the particular actions of racially motivated hatred or violence directed at people of color are symptomatic of something bigger is to say that racism in the United States is systemic. When I talk about racism being "systemic," I am talking about the ways in which racism is present within and throughout the entire system of our society and Church: in our laws, in our social hierarchies, in our storytelling and reporting, in our assumptions about one another, and in all other aspects of our context. As the sociologist Joe Feagin notes, the nature of systemic racism in the United States is distinctive because our country "is the only Western country that was explicitly founded on racial oppression."[3] When we truthfully consider the history of American society, from its founding by European colonists nearly half a millennium ago onward to today, we begin to see

---

2. Massingale, *Racial Justice and the Catholic Church*, 14.
3. Joe Feagin, *Systemic Racism: A Theory of Oppression* (New York: Routledge, 2006), 2.

that oppression based on race is not incidental to our shared social and ecclesial narrative. Instead, it is sadly a central and consistent element of our collective identity. It is most clearly recognized in the genocide of Indigenous people, the enslavement of Africans, and the mistreatment of immigrants. White people like me have been told and often tell others a version of American history that conveniently leaves out the painful truths of persistent oppression and violence against certain groups on account of their perceived race. We have been taught to ignore or dismiss the pervasiveness of racial oppression that touches every aspect of life in American society. And yet, women and men of color have lived through and still live with the devastating consequences of systemic racism.

To say that racism is systemic is to say that there is an accruing of consequences that arise from our unjust society. Over the centuries, white people have been free from the arbitrary and oppressive burdens experienced by people of color. Whereas Black people in this country were first enslaved and then systematically oppressed by legal and extralegal forms of injustice—segregation, lynching, voter suppression, imposed limits on housing, exclusion from financial investments, etc.—white people have been able to build intergenerational wealth and power. For generations white families have amassed material, economic, and political power; meanwhile, not only have Black families been excluded from similar opportunities, but much of the financial and social capital acquired by white people came at the expense of people of color. The way this unfolds in real time and over history can be very subtle and even imperceptible to most white people—that is, until we train ourselves to see *how* such social disparities between races originate and are maintained.

The Catholic faith has long been described as a "both/and" tradition as opposed to one that understands itself as "either/or." It doesn't take much effort to see why, for one only has to look at some of the basic beliefs expressed in our creeds and doctrines. Jesus Christ is *both* human *and* divine. Human beings are composed of *both* a material body *and* an immaterial soul. The elements of the Eucharist are *both* bread and wine *and* the sacramental presence of Christ. We could go on for a long time with more examples. However, it is precisely in this Catholic spirit of "both/and" that we need to approach the subject of racism. It is *both* the individual "commonsense" instances of racially motivated harm *and* it is a much larger and pervasive system of discrimination, oppression, and—for those who unwittingly benefit from the very same system—privilege. In order to understand better what is meant by the latter description of racism, Massingale suggests that we can think of the reality of systemic racism in terms of a "cultural phenomenon." He explains that, as a cultural phenomenon, racism is "a way of interpreting human color differences that pervades the collective convictions, conventions, and practices of American life. Racism functions as an ethos, as the animating spirit of US society, which lives on despite observable changes and assumes various incarnations in different historical circumstances."[4]

The thing about culture is that it is not easily identifiable. It is so present and so deeply ingrained as to become like second nature. Culture also shapes interpretation and meaning. Have you ever traveled abroad to a country very unlike your own? Think about the experience of spending time in a notably different culture. At first, things could seem to be very familiar, but upon closer examination you might start to notice

---

4. Massingale, *Racial Justice and the Catholic Church*, 15.

differences that strike you as "unusual." I remember the first time I visited England. While there are differences in spoken accents, currency, and the direction of traffic, there are a lot of things that appear at first similar between the United States and Great Britain. First among these is a shared language. But one doesn't have to be in a country like England long to realize that many of the everyday words and expressions that you and I take for granted in the United States have very different meanings overseas. Very quickly I realized that each country used terms differently, or different words to describe the same thing (there are many famous examples, such as "lift" instead of "elevator," "boot" instead of "trunk," "toilet" instead of "restroom").

But there were also more subtle differences that reflect unspoken cultural norms. For example, not only do the British drive cars on the left side of the road, but they also walk on the left side of the sidewalk (or "pavement" in England) and in the pedestrian tunnels of the subway system (or "the Underground" or simply "the Tube" in England). If you don't pick up quickly on those social cues, as I didn't the first time around, you might find yourself like I did, walking into oncoming pedestrian traffic and causing quite a chaotic scene during rush hour. There are other things, too, like where one sits in a taxi or rideshare vehicle, or how one orders food or drink in a pub, or what the polite or appropriate greeting is at a business or social event. Even in places that seem very familiar at first glance—like England and the United States—there are very subtle and numerous cultural differences that can be unsettling, exhausting, confusing, and unnerving. To many visitors in foreign countries, such differences are commonly presumed to be "odd," "different," or even "strange."

Where does that interpretation of an experience of another place and people come from? It comes from our culture, and it is reinforced by the very same, often invisible, dynamics. The way that cultures operate is yet another instance of a "both/and"—culture can *both* operate largely unseen *and* be always already everywhere. Massingale explains that cultures are shared, learned, formative, and symbolic.[5] As shared, a culture is never an individual person's perspectives, outlook, or imagination alone. There is something common to a particular group or society in which the culture is operating that signals normative values and ways of being that do not have to be spoken, but are intuitive and simply understood even in a nonconscious way.

As learned, a culture is passed on to each new member of the given society in both formal and informal ways. Think about the various preferences that arise in a given community. Oftentimes when we find ourselves in a new group, whether at school or church or work or somewhere else, there are intuitive cues and unspoken rules about "how we do things here" that are picked up without clear instruction. I think about the kinds of music I liked as a teenager. I was in a predominantly white cultural context at a private Catholic high school in the mid- to late 1990s. Among the most popular music that my friends and classmates listened to at the time was music by the Dave Matthews Band, which is exactly what I listened to as well. Nobody gave me a course or an instruction manual that told me that I should listen to or should like DMB, but I did and it reflected one small aspect of the cultural milieu of my experience. How about you? Did somebody sit you down and quiz you over what music choices, hairstyle, clothing options, or television programs are popular or reflective of the perspectives and values of your particular community? Likely not. But like

---

[5]. Massingale, *Racial Justice and the Catholic Church*, 16–17.

me, you also *learned* these things, sometimes through explicit instruction, but most times through observation and interaction with others.

As formative, a culture shapes one's way of seeing the world and existing in the world. Those aspects of the culture learned over time condition "our thoughts, values, and actions."[6] And, as symbolic, a culture is expressed in representative ways. Massingale notes that "culture is carried and expressed through visible markers (for example, art, music, language, clothing, literature, and dance)."[7] What people in a given cultural context believe to be attractive or preferable or ideal is shaped and evaluated according to the symbolic nature of culture. These symbols operate on multiple levels, and they both reflect and reinforce the learning and formative process of the culture itself. Our mannerisms and other subtle behaviors—such as speech patterns, colloquial terminology, and accents—both reflect our cultural formation and also help to reinforce these particular ways of seeing the world.

This brings us back to the matter of racism as a cultural phenomenon. The question we have to ask is, "*What kind* of culture is racism?" The answer to this question rests in the consequences of this generally subtle and sometimes overt system of cultural sharing, learning, formation, and symbols. Racism is a culture that justifies inequality and disparity between people identified according to their perceived race. For Black people and other people of color, the constant consequences of existing in a racist culture such as we have in the United States mean various degrees of oppression, marginalization, dismissal, harm, inequality, invisibility, disenfranchisement, and even threats to

---

6. Massingale, *Racial Justice and the Catholic Church*, 17.
7. Massingale, *Racial Justice and the Catholic Church*, 17.

life and safety. For whites, the consequences of existing in the same racist culture include a presumption that our experience of the world is the universal default—that the ideal or standard by which all are judged in the media, in person, in the classroom, at a police traffic stop, on the street, and in church is based on the prioritization of the appearance, values, success, and comfort of white people. This very real dynamic is what we call "white privilege," and it exists *everywhere* in the American ethos, including the Catholic Church.

This is illustrated well by the liturgy professor Kim Harris, who reflected on the ways that Black Catholics in general, and Black Catholic women in particular, feel unwelcomed by white Catholics. Harris explains that white Catholics often "feel uncomfortable with our Black Catholic bodies in nearby pews, our Black song presented for full and active participation by the assembly, our Black Catholic leaders as preachers, catechists, priests, deacons, religious sisters and brothers, and our Black worship cultures on equal footing within our historical Catholic worship cultures."[8] Too often our churches, like other public spaces, become locations where white cultural assumptions are presented as the default and standard way of doing things, thereby making anything different seem "odd," "wrong," or even "disrespectful." In the American Catholic context, songs, prayers, gestures, movements, preaching styles, and the like are considered "traditional" when they reflect a staid European sensibility and aesthetic. When this white cultural perspective is presumed to be absolute, and reinforced by white Church leaders and laity who hold power in the community, then other equally

---

8. Kim R. Harris, "Black Lives Matter in the Worshipping Church," *National Catholic Reporter*, July 10, 2020, https://www.ncronline.org/news/opinion/black-lives-matter-worshipping-church.

legitimate forms of worship and theological reflection are rejected and dismissed as "inappropriate." This is an example of racism and one that reflects its nuanced, subtle, and cultural nature.

There Is No Such Thing as "Reverse Racism"

One of the most common refrains I hear from other white people when I talk about racism and white privilege with them is an objection to the claim that only whites can be "racist." Inevitably, someone will raise the question: "What about *reverse racism*?" Typically such an objection will be followed with examples they believe illustrate how various high-profile people of color are, to their minds, "racist" against white people. Some of the examples invoked might even refer to particular Black women and men who might have publicly stated that they even "hate white people." The query is simple: Isn't this *also* a form of racism—a kind of "reverse racism"?

The simple answer is *no*.

The more complicated answer has everything to do with what we just discussed in terms of racism meaning a lot more than individual instances of racially motivated animus that we called the "commonsense" approach. Racism, properly speaking, refers to a whole system and culture, structures and institutions, laws and their enforcement, practices and perspectives that shape an entire society and the Church that exists in the very same world. The painful truth about the actual system and culture in the United States is that it is based on a dynamic that systematically disadvantages some people and advantages others according to their perceived race, and this has been the case since at least the genocide of native peoples living on this continent by European colonizers and the establishment of an economy dependent on the enslavement of African women and men. The uncomfortable fact that white people must come to terms with—and which people of color already know far clearer and more painfully than any white person could ever know—is that racism in this sense is only unidirectional; it does not "reverse."

To understand that dynamic and the absurdity of claims about so-called reverse racism (and, actually, doesn't that phrase itself reveal at least a presumption of a primary direction in order to suggest that it can change course or reverse?) requires that we appreciate the differences between "prejudice" motivated by race and "racism" as such.

Everyone, regardless of their social location, religious affiliation, gender, or racial identity, has prejudices. Robin DiAngelo, a racial justice advocate, explains, "Prejudice is pre-judgment about another person based on the social groups to which that person belongs. Prejudice consists of thoughts and feelings, including stereotypes, attitudes, and generalizations that are based on little or no experience and then are projected onto everyone from that group."[9] It is indeed possible for any particular social group to hold unfair or negatively biased judgments about another group. Such is the case in what people are identifying when they make claims about "reverse racism" or discriminatory prejudices aimed at white people by Black people and other people of color. Yes, Black people can hold prejudices about or even discriminate (that is, act in ways motivated by prejudice) against white people, but that's still *not racism*. The reason has everything to do with the larger social context in which this prejudice takes place. And since the laws, practices, institutions, and structures of American society have historically disempowered Black people, the support of cultural and

---

[9]. Robin DiAngelo, *White Fragility: Why It's So Hard for White People to Talk about Racism* (Boston: Beacon Press, 2018), 19.

systemic power does not work in their favor nor support deleterious effects of their potential prejudices in the same way that whites consistently experience.

DiAngelo summarizes the relationship between power and racism well. She writes: "When a racial group's collective prejudice is backed by the power of legal authority and institutional control, it is transformed into racism, a far-reaching system that functions independently from the intentions or self-images of individual actors."[10] In order for something to be "racist," it must be tied to a system of oppression like that found in the United States. Such systems are structured in a manner that allows the dominant group to disproportionately hold power and maintain the status quo in terms of policies and institutional structures that benefit those in the dominant group, those who hold the power. The function of power—and who holds and benefits from social, political, economic, and ecclesial power—is the determining factor. This is something Ijeoma Oluo includes in a very concise and direct definition of racism, offered in contrast to the overly simplistic and "commonsense" understanding. She states: "Racism is any prejudice against someone because of their race, when those views are reinforced by systems of power."[11] We cannot properly understand what is meant by racism without understanding the power dynamics always already at play in our nation and in our Church. Sure, it is hypothetically possible to imagine an alternative universe and history in which people of color disproportionately hold the power, oppress whites, and benefit from all the advantages afforded by a system of racial oppression and injustice. But that is pure fiction, an absolute

---

10. DiAngelo, *White Fragility*, 20.
11. Ijeoma Oluo, *So You Want to Talk about Race* (New York: Seal Press, 2019), 26.

counterfactual. Phrases such as "reverse racism" distract from the violent and painful truth of history and its contemporary consequences. When white people defensively invoke such claims as "reverse racism," we end up proposing a false equivalency—the possibility of racial prejudice for the reality of systemic racism—and reinforce our own willful ignorance and desire to live comfortably with the lie that to be racist or experience racism is only ever a series of isolated, individual, and infrequent events. Therefore, we feel that we can exonerate ourselves because we may never have participated in such a "racist event."

But when we begin to see the larger picture of racism as a system or culture, we can see how our society is rigged in such a way as to limit the opportunities for true equity and justice for Black people from the outset. The examples are too numerous to name exhaustively here, but it is worth naming a few examples. Take, for instance, the fact that Black people, who make up approximately 13 percent of the national population, are more than twice as likely to be killed by police than white people, who make up approximately 60 percent of the national population.[12] Another horrifying example that results in a disproportionate amount of unnecessary mortality is the racial disparity in pregnancy-related deaths in the United States. According to a 2019 Centers for Disease Control and Prevention report, Black women are *three times more likely* than white women to die as a result of complications with pregnancy or childbirth.[13] What makes this a particularly disturbing statistic is that medical

---

12. See the "Fatal Force" database, *Washington Post*, accessed September 10, 2020, https://www.washingtonpost.com/graphics/investigations/police-shootings-database/.

13. Emily E. Petersen et al., "Racial/Ethnic Disparities in Pregnancy-Related Deaths—United States, 2007–2016," *Morbidity and Mortality Weekly Report* 68 (September 6, 2019): 762–65.

professionals explain that most pregnancy-related deaths are preventable. The reason such a disproportionate number of Black women and other women of color die has little to do with the inherent dangers of pregnancy and everything to do with the health-care system in the United States and how it treats people of color. Limited access to health-care treatment and facilities, the lack of attention or personal care provided by medical staff to patients of color, the inequality of insurance coverage, and the growing costs of medical care in the United States all reflect the consequences of a culturally racist system. For Catholics, these are particularly compelling signs of racial injustice given that we pride ourselves on being a "pro-life" community. Racism is not merely an abstract idea but a reality that has life-or-death consequences for Black women and children.

Additionally, there are also many other less immediately fatal illustrations of systemic racial injustice. Consider the disparity in white versus Black household median wealth. According to a 2017 Federal Reserve report, Black families have a median and mean net worth that is less than 15 percent of the median and mean net worth of white households.[14] The astonishing gap between white and Black people regarding household wealth is indicative of the generations of opportunities Black women and men had been blocked from accessing. From the illegal practice of banks' and real estate agents' redlining in the twentieth century—which is the practice of deliberately withholding mortgages and access to

---

14. Lisa J. Dettling et al., "Recent Trends in Wealth-Holding by Race and Ethnicity: Evidence from the Survey of Consumer Finances," *FEDS Notes* (Washington, DC: Board of Governors of the Federal Reserve System, September 2017), https://www.federalreserve.gov/econres/notes/feds-notes/recent-trends-in-wealth-holding-by-race-and-ethnicity-evidence-from-the-survey-of-consumer-finances-20170927.htm.

certain neighborhoods on account of one's race—to the continued gap in wages earned and job opportunities available in our own time, Black people are routinely disadvantaged by the very social structures, policies, and laws from which the white population has consistently benefited.

When it comes to the wage gap, the difference between what white and Black people earn on average has actually *increased*, meaning that Black women and men working the same jobs actually make *less* on average compared to white women and men. According to a 2017 report from the Bureau of Labor Statistics, in 1979 Black men earned on average 80 percent of what a white man earned in the same job. However, in 2016, after factoring in inflation and other variables, Black men only made on average a startling 70 percent of what their white counterparts were making. For women, the decline is even starker. Black women in 1979 made an average of 95 percent of what white women made, whereas in 2016 that percentage dropped to 82 percent.[15] Interestingly, the authors of this report attribute this racial earnings gap to "unexplained factors," though it is apparent to those familiar with the historical deprivation of opportunities and equity in the American workforce that systemic racism is the clearest explanation. Perhaps the reason why it is so challenging for many white people to recognize the role of racism behind data points like these is because most white people have convinced ourselves that racism is limited to discrete acts of violence or hatred, and therefore widespread cultural disparities such as those found in employment or housing don't fit comfortably into that misleadingly narrow frame.

---

15. Eleni X. Karageorge, "The Unexplainable, Growing Black-White Wage Gap," *Monthly Labor Review*, November 17, 2017, https://www.bls.gov/opub/mlr/2017/beyond-bls/the-unexplainable-growing-black-white-wage-gap.htm.

In addition to the systemic issues like these that must be named, what is not included in the "commonsense" understanding of racism as discrete acts is the equally pervasive reality of white privilege. This concept is particularly challenging for many white people to see and even harder for them to accept because it effectively pulls the rug out from beneath individuals who have convinced themselves of the lies of American meritocracy and independent success. People of goodwill can easily unite with one another to name and condemn overt acts of racially motivated animus—this or that instance of "commonsense racism"—because our society and Church respects and even sometimes rewards those who call out violence, harm, and injustice. What is much, much more difficult is turning the investigatory gaze back on ourselves as white people to see how there exist centuries-old structures of racial oppression and disenfranchisement that have benefited and *continue* to benefit white people, regardless of whatever other hardships an individual or particular group of white people in the United States might experience.

It is also worth noting that when we talk about the structure of racism and its unidirectional flow of harm and benefits—the former to people of color, the latter to whites—we are not just talking about numerical minorities and majorities. As was globally recognized in the 1980s and 1990s, the apartheid rule of South Africa by its numerical minority white population resulted in exactly this racist dynamic that explicitly burdened and oppressed its Black numerical majority population for decades. It's never just about numbers; it's always about power—who has it, who benefits from it, who doesn't, and why. A similar phenomenon has been operative in the United States from before our nation's founding, but the structure of racism has facilitated the denial of its reality by white people because of the mechanisms of cover-up and dismissal that white privilege inherently produces (we'll explore how this works in greater detail in the next chapter). The irony that whites in the American context responded more readily to the injustices of apartheid South Africa and its systemic racism than to those egregious racial injustices here at home calls to mind the admonition of Jesus in Matthew's gospel about the hypocrisy of those quick to point out the speck in the eyes of others while ignoring the wooden beam protruding from their own (see Matthew 7:3–5). One of the ways that white Catholics, in particular, can begin to address this hypocrisy in our own lives is by surrendering the baseless attempts to defend ourselves when confronted with the incontrovertible truth of systemic racism. We must allow ourselves to be vulnerable, to experience the discomfort of an uncomfortable truth, because only then will we be able to begin the work of addressing the reality of racism in our lives, communities, nation, and Church.

The simple fact remains that in the United States, based on our actual history, only white society can be racist.[16] Even while white people may in exceptional circumstances find themselves the individual object of somebody else's prejudice, the cultural, legal, and ecclesial power ultimately supports those in the place of social dominance—and in the American context,

---

[16.] Indeed, within a white society there are other populations that both benefit from and are simultaneously oppressed by systemic racism. A good example of this phenomenon is seen in the experience of the Latinx community, which has historically struggled in the United States both with their own anti-Black racism and with being the objects of anti-immigration and anti-Brown racism. For more, see J. D. Long-García, "How Latino Catholics Are Grappling with Their Own History of Racism," *America*, August 31, 2020, https://www.americamagazine.org/politics-society/2020/08/31/latinos-racism-catholic-church.

that is white people. As DiAngelo explains, "When I say that only whites can be racist, I mean that in the United States, only whites have the collective social and institutional power and privilege over people of color. People of color do not have this power and privilege over white people."[17] As the historian Ibram Kendi notes, "Denial is the heartbeat of racism, beating across ideologies, races, and nations. It is beating within us."[18] As white Catholics, we must confront this denial within our own hearts. We must recognize that like our actual beating hearts—which do not draw our conscious attention at most moments of most days during most of our lives, but nevertheless are there, real, and beating—so too the reality of racial injustice and the effects of a systemic racism are present deep within each of us. The aim of this book is to help white Catholics recognize that problematic heartbeat, perhaps for the first time, in order to address it directly. Real change is neither quick nor easy, but everyone has to start somewhere.

Further Reading

- Eduardo Bonilla-Silva, *Racism without Racists: Color-Blind Racism and the Persistence of Racial Inequality in America*, 5th ed. (Lanham, MD: Rowman & Littlefield, 2018).
- Richard Delgado and Jean Stefancic, *Critical Race Theory: An Introduction,* 2nd ed. (New York: New York University Press, 2012).
- Robin DiAngelo, *White Fragility: Why It's So Hard for White People to Talk about Racism* (Boston: Beacon Books, 2019).

---

[17]. DiAngelo, *White Fragility*, 22.
[18]. Ibram X. Kendi, *How to Be an Antiracist* (New York: One World, 2019), 9.

- Michael Eric Dyson, *Tears We Cannot Stop: A Sermon to White America* (New York: St. Martin's Press, 2017).
- Joe R. Feagin, *Systemic Racism: A Theory of Oppression* (New York: Routledge, 2006).
- bell hooks, *Writing beyond Race: Living Theory and Practice* (New York: Routledge, 2013).
- Ibram X. Kendi, *How to Be an Antiracist* (New York: One World, 2019).
- Ibram X. Kendi, *Stamped from the Beginning: The Definitive History of Racist Ideas in America* (New York: Nation Books, 2016).
- Bryan N. Massingale, *Racial Justice and the Catholic Church* (Maryknoll, NY: Orbis Books, 2010).
- Ijeoma Oluo, *So You Want to Talk about Race* (New York: Seal Press, 2019).
- Isabel Wilkerson, *Caste: The Origins of Our Discontents* (New York: Random House, 2020).

2

What Does It Mean to Be White?

Recently, a white friend of mine shared with me a transformative experience she had while in middle school. She conveyed that one summer day she and one of her close friends were walking along the sidewalk in the affluent and predominantly white neighborhood where they both grew up outside of Seattle. As she recounted, they were engrossed in conversation as people walked past them and traffic drove by, and then suddenly they were stopped in their tracks. A glass bottle, seemingly arriving from nowhere, shattered on the sidewalk just a few steps in front of them. Frightened and caught off guard, they looked around to see where this had come from as a truck sped away with the driver shouting at them something they couldn't quite make out.

My friend recalled decades later that she then turned, confused and upset, to her friend and said: "He threw a bottle at us! Why would someone do something like that?" And, without missing a beat, her middle-school friend replied: "It's probably because I'm Black."

In telling this experience to me, my friend remembered how matter-of-fact her friend's response was to her. As a Black girl in an overwhelmingly white and affluent suburb, she was all too aware of the way racism functions in society, including in seemingly progressive locations like the Pacific Northwest. All these years later, my friend remembers the feeling of a personal revelation about race and racial injustice. She told me: "Instantly and for the very first time, I realized that she was Black and I was white. Of course we had noticed and discussed the differences in our skin color before this incident. What I mean is that, for the first time, I glimpsed what the difference our races meant for our everyday experiences of the world."

This experience of realizing the disparities that racial difference occasions in the United States led my friend to consider not only the unjust effects of racism on her young Black friend but also the ways her own whiteness impacts and influences her understanding of the world. They had grown up in the same suburban community, attended the same public schools, and moved within the same circle of friends, and yet there was another consciousness that her Black friend was forced to confront from an early age. It was awareness that the color of her skin could, at any moment, occasion random acts of hatred and even violence. My friend explained: "That she immediately assumed her Blackness might be the reason for the driver's actions made this clear to me. In contrast, I, as a white girl, grew up assuming the benevolence of others. I never once thought about how my skin color might affect the behavior of others. It certainly never crossed my mind that it could rouse aggression from strangers."

Learning about whiteness can be a startling reality for many white people because we white people in the United States have been generally raised, socialized, taught, entertained, and informed by a system that casts doubt on the existence of whiteness as a racial category itself and, in the rare instance in which whiteness is acknowledged, denies it has any meaningful consequence. To learn about our assumed racial identity when so much effort and energy have gone into denying it, ignoring it, or explaining it away is to risk encountering the manifold falsehoods that whites have taken for granted as truth. It means risking the discomfort of knowing what has been invisible to you but plain to people of color, as well as having to relearn a fair amount about reality and to forgo faulty assumptions about *who* we are and *how* we are in a world marred by inescapable racism and white supremacy.

Because the reality of anti-Black racism in the United States is typically invisible to most whites by virtue of the racial blind spots reinforced by white privilege, we cannot trust our own uncritical instincts about racism in general and whiteness in particular. Awareness of this kind of distance between perception and reality has regularly led to white people playing down the seriousness of racial injustice or ascribing discrete acts of racist violence to isolated circumstances. What this widespread pattern amounts to is the unwillingness of many white people to listen to and believe what Black women and men have been saying for years about their experience. There have been some white women and men, however, who have tried very hard to understand the experience of Black people in America. The white writer John Howard Griffin attempted one of the more famous and extreme instances of such an effort in 1959.

With the assistance of a dermatologist from New Orleans, Griffin took medication that changed the pigmentation of his skin to a dark hue, resulting in his presenting as a Black man. Griffin's project, motivated in part by his Catholic conviction about the inherent dignity and value of all people, sought to allow him to feel what it was like to live the day-to-day experience of being a Black man in the American South during the 1950s. The experience, which was conveyed in the book

Black Like Me in 1962, terrified Griffin as much as it informed him.[1] In a way most other white people would never know, Griffin spent the fall of 1959 traveling in the Deep South—Louisiana, Mississippi, Alabama, and Georgia—experiencing the world in an entirely new and unfamiliar way to him. Fear looms large in his telling of the events, because it was frightening to be Black in the segregated South where lynchings routinely took the lives of innocent men and boys, oftentimes occasioned only by the rumor or suspicion of a sideways glance or impure thought about a white person. He was for the first time the target of racial slurs, overtly dismissive and rude behavior, and discrimination in forms too numerous to recount here.

Griffin became a more credible narrator of the experience of racism in the United States than most white people because of his unusual, risky, and extreme project. However, despite the harrowing instances of his being the target of racist animosity and the persistent precariousness of being perceived as a Black man in the Jim Crow South, he nevertheless retained the privilege of eventually returning to his normal state of whiteness, something the Black women and men he met and who cared for him along his journey would never have the opportunity to pursue. This is not to suggest that he did not suffer consequences for what he experienced and courageously conveyed in interviews, articles, and *Black Like Me*. Indeed, he and his family had to flee to Mexico from their home in Texas because of persistent death threats from fellow whites.[2] What was so powerful about Griffin's journey was the way in which he came to experience firsthand, as much as a white man could, what his Black brothers and

---

[1] John Howard Griffin, *Black Like Me* (New York: Penguin Books, 1962).

[2] Bruce Watson, "Black Like Me, 50 Years Later," *Smithsonian Magazine*, October 2019.

sisters lived with daily. It taught him not only about Blackness in America but about the privileges and ignorance his whiteness occasioned.

But one does not have to go to such physical extremes to learn about the realities of racism and white privilege. The problem in Griffin's time—as it continues to be a problem in our own—is that white people *did not listen to*, let alone *believe*, what Black people were telling them about the world and the injustices of our society. Even Griffin's action suggests that he could not fully accept the word of his Black sisters and brothers until he, in the spirit of the doubting apostle Thomas after Jesus' resurrection, saw the evils of racism with his own (white) eyes and in his own (darkened) skin. There is a lot to commend about Griffin's captivatingly written personal narrative of what anti-Black racism is like in his rare experience, but it also puts into stark relief the important need for white people to listen to, learn from, and sincerely incorporate what people of color, who suffer most the consequences of racial injustice, have said and continue to say about the realities of race in the United States.

We white people are, at least at first, unreliable narrators about race. Women and men of color, however, have long attested to the painful truths of racism and privilege in a white supremacist culture, and they have accurately narrated the basic aspects of what it means to be white within such a context. They can do this because their experience, at nearly every point of navigating life in a pervasively racist society, is one of encountering subjugation, minimization, dismissal, and rejection—all against a contrast of "whiteness" presented as normative, which people of color have never had the privilege to overlook or ignore. When scholars and activists talk about the United States being a "white supremacist" nation, this is at the heart of that forceful, yet true, summation. Though many people assume that "white supremacist" is a term reserved for only those who avowedly embrace the belief of white racial superiority, like racism in general, the term "white supremacy" is far more nuanced. Because the American cultural context is one in which whiteness is presumed to be the default in all aspects of life, our society is rightly described as one that elevates those people and things associated with whiteness while subordinating or denigrating those people or things associated with any other racial identity.

I have learned from and been challenged by the insightful work of many people of color who are far more reliable narrators about whiteness than even the most self-critically aware white person. And I continue to learn and be humbled by my own ignorance and deeply ingrained racism. To put it bluntly, most white people in the United States do not know who we are because, as the writer James Baldwin observed, whites live a lie of their own creation and support the perpetuation of the lie of neutrality, normalcy, and supremacy by means of opposition and "othering."[3] White identity is often framed as: "I am *not x*," or "I am *not y*," and so on. According to this formulation, to ask, "What does it mean to be white?" leads to the inevitable,

---

[3]. See James Baldwin, "On Being White . . . and Other Lies," in *The Cross of Redemption: Uncollected Writings*, ed. Randall Kenan (New York: Vintage Books, 2011), 166–70. Relatedly, see George Yancy, *Look, A White! Philosophical Essays on Whiteness* (Philadelphia: Temple University Press, 2012), 7: "Whites who choose to give their attention to thinking critically about whiteness are incapable of doing so, though it does mean that there will be structural blinkers that occlude specific and complex insights by virtue of being white." He adds: "People of color are necessary to the project of critically thinking through whiteness," particularly if we wish to avoid a kind of solipsism or "narcissistic project" that again makes everything simply and uncritically about white people.

if unspoken, response: "It means to be *not Black.*" This is an instance of what scholars call "social binaries," where individuals and groups form identities over against and in opposition to another group that is typically viewed by the dominant group as "lesser than" and inferior. This sort of dynamic is not limited to race as the only determining category, but applies across the board of systemic oppression; and each form of oppression has a title (sometimes collectively referred to as the "isms"). Some common examples in America include male/female (sexism), straight/LGBTQ (heterosexism), wealthy/poor (classism), able-bodied/disabled (ableism), and, of course, white/Black (racism).[4] As Harlon Dalton has summarized, "Race exists only in relation to one another. Whiteness is meaningless in the absence of Blackness; the same holds in reverse. Moreover, race itself would be meaningless if it were not a fault line along which power, prestige, and respect are distributed."[5] On this last point, it is worth noting that race is about meaning making in the American context. It is, on the one hand, an arbitrary system of valuation tied to appearances, perceptions, and external categories. However, that the system is arbitrary—that is, it doesn't have any objective grounding in science or anything else outside of particular social contexts—does not mean race is unimportant or irrelevant. On the contrary, because we live in a society that places an immense amount of significance on race, it is extremely consequential for both the beneficiaries (whites) and those who are harmed or disadvantaged by the same system (Blacks and other people of color).

---

[4]. See Robin DiAngelo, *What Does It Mean to Be White? Developing White Racial Literacy*, rev. ed. (New York: Peter Lang, 2016), 63–64.

[5]. Harlon Dalton, "Failing to See," in *White Privilege: Essential Readings on the Other Side of Racism*, ed. Paula S. Rothenberg, 5th ed. (New York: Macmillan, 2016), 16.

This chapter explores the meaning and experience of whiteness to better assist white women and men interested in understanding the complex reality of systemic racism in society and the Church. What follows is an introduction to the idea and experience of whiteness presented in four categories: as a social construct, as normative in the American context, as a kind of personal and collective property, and as unhelpfully manifested at times in terms of rage and fragility.

Whiteness as a Social Construct

Race as a human characteristic is socially constructed. This fact often strikes many people as odd or confusing, as if naming something a "social construct" is akin to saying "make believe" or "mythological" or "imaginary." This response, while incorrect, is nevertheless understandable given the way that race functions so prominently in overt and covert ways within American society. To say that something is a social construct is not to deny its veracity, but is actually a way of describing its origins and existence. We live in a world full of social constructions. For instance, take the case of a hexagon-shaped piece of metal painted red with the letters "S," "T," "O," and "P" written on it. With or without the letters present, anyone in the United States (and many other places), from a preliterate child to an elderly adult, can identify the meaning of that signage. We all know that it means "stop." But there is nothing intrinsic to the color red or a six-sided shape (hexagon) or even the letters that spell out the word "stop" that necessarily means the act of stopping when previously in motion. Street signs are social constructs. The meaning signified by a street sign exists as the result of a particular value applied ("construct") to it by a particular group of people ("social"), and there are certain rules and policies associated with that meaning that are understood by all members of that society. In the case of the street sign example, a specific society determined that a red hexagon sign placed alongside a road or intersection would mean "stop." Even though there is nothing scientifically objective or otherwise inherent to suggest that interpretation in the sign itself, that meaning is so well understood across the given society that it is immediately understood just by the appearance of a red hexagon alone.

A similar dynamic is at play when we talk about the meaning of race as a human characteristic. Certainly, I do not mean to suggest that human beings created in the image and likeness of God can be reduced to something as seemingly insignificant as a street sign. What I do want to emphasize is the manner in which a lot of things that people generally take for granted arise as a result of a particular meaning assigned by a society to arbitrary features of an object, person, or even whole communities. Just as the shape and color of a street sign are associated with its socially constructed meaning, so too when it comes to the physical appearance of particular groups of people, meaning is assigned and maintained by spoken and unspoken, written and unwritten rules, policies, structures, systems, assumptions, and prejudices. For some people in the American context, the perceived color of their skin is assumed to denote inferiority; such is the case with BIPOC. For others, the perceived color of their skin is assumed to denote superiority; such is the case with those categorized as white. In both cases, that which signals the valuation—phenotype, or the set of observable physical characteristics of a person—is arbitrary. It is conceivable that in a fictional alternative universe or course of history the assigned meaning to phenotype could be reversed, wherein those categorized as white would be disadvantaged while those categorized as Black would be advantaged by the same system.

A fictional illustration of what this alternative reality might look like was portrayed well in the 2018 Marvel movie *Black Panther*, in which the mythical land of Wakanda remains untouched by white colonialism and where white people do not hold socially privileged status. However, sadly, this is not the case in reality—history tells a painful and horrifying story about the persistent significance of race as a two-sided coin of systemic racism and white supremacy. And that history is one of the development and maintenance of Blackness and whiteness as social constructions that subordinated one group and elevated the other.

As the philosopher Charles W. Mills explains, "This racial dichotomization was not incidental. It was not just that the rulers happened to be white and the subjected happened to be nonwhite. Rather, race was absolutely central to the justificatory ideology of the period [of the eighteenth through twentieth centuries]. It was precisely *because* of alleged white superiority to other races that whites saw themselves as entitled to rule over them."[6] The meaning assigned to skin color or phenotype arose from a system of power, shaped in particular by the European colonization of what is today North America, beginning with the dislocation and genocide of the Indigenous peoples of this land and then the emergence of the Atlantic slave trade. Just as the meaning of Blackness (or, more bluntly, *non-whiteness*) developed and shifted in accordance with the historical circumstances of oppression and white supremacy over the last four centuries, so too did the meaning of whiteness, even if it was neither easily or deliberately recognized. As sociologist Teresa J. Guess explains,

> Social actors were involved in constructing laws, rules, and regulations that created structured social relations during Slavery, Reconstruction, Jim Crow, and the Civil

---

6. Charles W. Mills, "Global White Supremacy," *White Privilege*, 120.

Rights eras. Both black and *white* people, both enslaved and free people understood the racial rules that ordered their day-to-day routines in everyday life. Across time and space, racial routines in social interaction became institutionalized practices that ensured social distance and geographical separation between black and *white* population groups.[7]

Race is, as the renowned historian Nell Irvin Painter plainly states, "an idea, not a fact, and its questions demand answers from the conceptual rather than the factual realm."[8] To begin to understand what race is, one has to grapple with the history of a concept, an idea, and reckon with its fluidity.

Painter explains: "Constructions of whiteness have changed over time, shifting to accommodate the demands of social change. Before the mid-19th century, the existence of more than one white race was commonly accepted, in popular culture and scholarship."[9] Various groups of European immigrants—Irish, Italians, Jews from Eastern Europe, and so on—were considered as embodying various degrees of whiteness, which established a hierarchical casting of those who might today comfortably identify or be categorized as "white."[10] That there has always

---

[7]. Teresa J. Guess, "The Social Construction of Whiteness: Racism by Intent, Racism by Consequence," *Critical Sociology* 32, no. 4 (2006): 659, emphasis original.

[8]. Nell Irvin Painter, *The History of White People* (New York: W. W. Norton, 2010), ix.

[9]. Nell Irvin Painter, "What Is Whiteness?" *New York Times*, June 20, 2015.

[10]. For example, see David R. Roediger, *Working toward Whiteness: How America's Immigrants Became White* (New York: Basic Books, 2005); Matthew Frye Jacobson, *Whiteness of a Different Color: European Immigrants and the Alchemy of Race* (Cambridge, MA: Harvard University Press, 1998);

been a shifting sense to the meaning of race highlights what we mean when we talk about it as a social construct; it is something not determined by objective fact but by societal declaration.

Law professor Angela Onwuachi-Willig picks up on this insight about the fluidity and historical development of race in an effort to debunk the false belief that because race is about physical appearance it necessarily has its origins in biology. She writes: "Race is not biological. It is a social construct. There is no gene or cluster of genes common to all blacks or all whites. Were race 'real' in the genetic sense, racial classifications for individuals would remain constant across boundaries. Yet, a person who could be categorized as black in the United States might be considered white in Brazil or colored in South Africa."[11] For example, since the early twentieth century, Brazil has categorized its population according to six racial groups: Branco ("White"), Pardo ("Brown" or "Mixed Race"), Preto ("Black"), Cabaclo (another form of "Mixed Race"), Amarelo ("Asian"), and Indigenous peoples. Given Brazil's own social history and cultural background, these categories do not easily align with what is generally categorized as "Black" or "white" in the US context.[12] Likewise, the racial categorization in South

---

and Karen Brodkin, *How Jews Became White Folks and What That Says about Race in America* (New Brunswick, NJ: Rutgers University Press, 1994).

11. Angela Onwuachi-Willig, "Race and Racial Identity Are Social Constructs," Room for Debate Series, *New York Times*, updated September 6, 2016, https://www.nytimes.com/roomfordebate/2015/06/16/how-fluid-is-racial-identity/race-and-racial-identity-are-social-constructs.

12. For example, see Mara Loveman, Jeronimo O. Muniz, and Stanley R. Bailey, "Brazil in Black and White? Race Categories, the Census, and the Study of Inequality," *Ethnic and Racial Studies* 35 (2012): 1466–83; and Cleuci de Oliveira, "Brazil's New Problem with Blackness," *Foreign Policy*, April 5, 2017, https://foreignpolicy.com/2017/04/05/brazils-new-problem-with-blackness-affirmative-action/.

Africa, which consists of the labels African, Coloured (generally those of "Mixed Race"), White, and Asian, does not easily align with other phenotypical categories in other social contexts.[13] Racial classification is contextual and arbitrary.

Robin DiAngelo adds:

> The idea of race as biological makes it easy to believe that many of the divisions we see in society are natural. But race . . . is socially constructed. The differences we *do see* with our eyes, such as hair texture and eye color, are superficial and emerged as adaptations to geography; there really is no race under the skin. The differences we *believe* we see ([e.g.,] Lakisha is less qualified than Emily, or Jamal is more prone to violence) are a result of our socialization; our racial lenses. While there is no biological race as we understand it, race as a *social construction* has profound significance and impacts every aspect of our lives.[14]

This recognition of what scholars call "scientific racism," those tenuous linkages between race and biology, is an important starting point for conversations about race and racism in the United States. We have to disabuse ourselves of this false justification for the unjust systems of advantage and disadvantage that are based on assigning meaning to something as arbitrary as

---

13. See George T. H. Ellison and Thea de Wet, "The Classification of South Africa's Mixed-Heritage Peoples, 1910–2011: A Century of Conflation, Contradiction, Containment, and Contention," in *The Palgrave International Handbook of Mixed Racial and Ethnic Classification*, ed. Zarine L. Rocha and Peter J. Aspinall (New York: Palgrave Macmillan, 2020), 425–55.

14. DiAngelo, *What Does It Mean to Be White?*, 98.

skin color or appearance, which has had long-standing historical consequences. When we talk about race, we have to recall that there is a deeply complex social and institutional context that undergirds and reinforces certain power relations, identity formation, and assumptions; this context is associated with how one appears physically with regard to certain spoken and unspoken cultural norms.

Whiteness is one among many socially constructed races in our American context, but most of us white folks have been conditioned to view ourselves as nonracialized and therefore "normal," "natural," and "default" in relationship to others who are not white. Realizing the truth about the arbitrariness of racial classification and its lack of biological grounding helps us to see the world with greater clarity and nuance. If we white people allow ourselves to continue learning, over time our awareness of the meaning applied to and consequences arising from racial categorization will increase and our ability to recognize the two-sided coin of racial injustice and white privilege will improve.

Whiteness as Normative

During my first year of formation as a Franciscan friar, at a stage of religious life called "postulancy," I lived with my five classmates at a parish in the South Bronx that predominantly served the large Hispanic communities in the area. The Spanish-language liturgies were always packed, full of energy, and reflecting the whole range of life from young families with newborn infants to great-grandmothers serving as anchors of the faith community. This was the first time that I was living and ministering in a setting where my racial (white) and ethnic (Irish American) identities were clearly in the minority. Because of the complex history and nature of American racism that reserves its most harsh treatment for Black people, however, the contrast between my previous two decades of life living in predominantly white communities and what I was experiencing in the Bronx did not seem as jarring as I might have thought. But I was aware that my lack of Spanish fluency and my Latinx cultural naïveté put me in a new kind of heightened personal awareness of the color of my skin, the sound of my voice, the style of my clothing, and the cultural norms I presumed. For perhaps the first sustained time in my life, I was confronted by and aware of my whiteness.

This awareness was occasioned by the social contrast I encountered not only in the parish and in the community but also within the friary. To be sure, the local community of Franciscan friars was overwhelmingly composed of whites. But two of my five classmates were from countries in Central and South America, and one of them, originally from Peru, used to tease me in a lighthearted manner that called out my whiteness in a way I had not experienced before. He used to say, often apropos of nothing in particular, "Dan, you're not ethnic. You're just white." I recall at first being thrown off guard by this joking around, feeling on one hand that I had to "defend" myself, that there was something of a subtle insult behind the remark. Early on in our time as classmates I would put up a minor protest to the effect of, "What are you talking about? I'm Irish on both sides of my family; that's an ethnicity! We Irish have millennia-old culture!" My defense was weak because I wasn't always sure why I was feeling the need to be defensive or what was actually being triggered in me by that kind of remark.

But over time I began to understand better what my classmate was signaling. Despite the fact that he came from a very high-class and powerful family back in Peru (his father was a senior government official, he had been educated at the best schools, he spoke English with hardly an accent, etc.), in the context of the United States he was generally categorized by the color of his skin, the country of his origin, and the language of his family. What his joking with me drew on was the normative status of whiteness in the American context, which predicated "color" and "ethnicity" and "otherness" and "difference" only to those who were *non-whites*. The joke was funny in part because it was the reversal of racist minoritizing, which often homogenized people of color into an indistinguishable group rather than a collection of unique persons. Individuality and agency were reserved, as a default, for whites like me in American society. But the joke with its playful reversal on racial dynamics only makes sense in light of the painful reality of white normativity, which is a central part of systemic racism and white supremacy. My classmate understood that dynamic all too well, and it was something that I had to learn and could only really begin to see honestly through the experiences of those not presumed to be part of the "white norm."

White women and men do not generally talk about whiteness because the dynamics that make possible the burdening and oppression of persons of color also simultaneously cover over the reality of "whiteness" as a racial marker within this web of relations. This is why it didn't occur to me right away what was so funny about my classmate's joke. As a result of this dynamic always already at work, that which is perceived to be "white" is viewed to be normative, neutral, acceptable, ordinary, the default, or the ideal. As we already saw, because it is socially constructed, those who are considered "white" vary with time. Bryan Massingale has explained, "It is important to note that 'white' is a fluid category that has come to include over the years ethnic groups from other parts of the world" beyond those of

Western European descent.[15] The historical record of shifting admission to the social category of "white" itself should further trouble any assumption of an objective, static, or scientific grounding for race. But what is consistent is that all things considered "white," whether people or perspective or culture, are considered to be superior and normative in a racist society.

Philosopher Sara Ahmed further highlights that whites do not generally recognize whiteness because they are socialized to believe that their identities, perspectives, and cultures are simply the norm or default—that is, *the way things ought to be*. "It has become commonplace for whiteness to be represented as invisible, as the unseen or the unmarked, as non-color, the absent presence or hidden referent, against which all other colors are measured as forms of deviance."[16] There is perhaps no clearer illustration of this white normativity in practice than the first-aid aisle of most pharmacies and supermarkets. While a few exceptions have appeared in recent years, bandages are often described as "flesh color" or "nude," something that is also endemic in the cosmetic and clothing industry. But whose "flesh color" is being described here? It's almost never shades reflecting the skin of people of color. Instead, it is a light-toned, pinkish-tan color aimed at buyers of fair or even pallid complexion. In other words, when bandage, cosmetic, clothing, and other companies think "flesh" or "skin," they think *white*.

To be white is to be normative and without need for a qualifier in this society. As the theorist George Lipsitz explains, "Whiteness is everywhere in U.S. culture, but it is very hard to see. . . . As

---

[15]. Bryan N. Massingale, *Racial Justice and the Catholic Church* (Maryknoll, NY: Orbis Books, 2010), 2.

[16]. Sara Ahmed, "Declarations of Whiteness: The Non-Performativity of Anti-Racism," *borderlands e-journal* 3 (2004), http://www.borderlands.net.au/vol3no2_2004/ahmed_declarations.htm.

the unmarked category against which difference is constructed, whiteness never has to speak its name, never has to acknowledge its rule as an organizing principle in social and cultural relations."[17] To sum up the blindness to the reality of whiteness as experienced by most white people, George Yancy explains:

> The fact of the matter is that, for white people, whiteness is the transcendental norm in terms of which they live their lives as persons, individuals. People of color, however, confront whiteness in their everyday lives, not as an abstract concept but in the form of embodied whites who engage in racist practices that negatively affect their lives. Black people and people of color thus strive to disarticulate the link between whiteness and the assumption of just being human, to create a critical slippage.[18]

Elsewhere, Yancy likens the socialization of whites into whiteness to the manner in which native English speakers learn English growing up: "One learns English in the context of the everyday by hearing it spoken. The 'subject' of the language-learning process does not self-consciously incorporate the grammar of English. Yet parents engage in correcting the linguistic performances of their children; this is part of what it means to inhabit a linguistic community."[19] Likewise, white people inhabit a racialized community in which they "become white" through subtle, uncritical, and tacit socialization. At times there are stronger signals sent to "correct" the "racial

---

17. George Lipsitz, *The Possessive Investment in Whiteness: How White People Profit from Identity Politics*, rev. ed. (Philadelphia: Temple University Press, 2006), 1.
18. Yancy, *Look! A White!*, 7.
19. Yancy, *Look, A White!*, 24–25.

grammar" of white performance, but oftentimes it goes without saying.

Because white people have been formed to think of ourselves and our experiences as normative for reality, it can be very difficult for us to see the truth. As Yancy stated and my classmate experienced, this is not the case for people of color, who are continuously confronted with messages—subtle and explicit—that they are not "normal," they are "different," they are "other" or, euphemistically, "*ethnic*." This is something that the scholar and civil rights activist W. E. B. Du Bois understood personally and academically, when in 1903 he described the presence of a "double-consciousness" that Black people experience when confronted with the structural, institutional, and historical realities of American racism and white normativity. He wrote: "It is a peculiar sensation, this double-consciousness, this sense of always looking at one's self through the eyes of others, of measuring one's soul by the tape of a world that looks on in amused contempt and pity. One ever feels his twoness—an American, a Negro; two souls, two thoughts, two un-reconciled strivings; two warring ideals in one dark body, whose dogged strength alone keeps it from being torn asunder."[20]

Du Bois's reflection on the effects of the normative "white gaze" on his black body anticipates the reflections of the political philosopher Frantz Fanon a half century later, who likewise calls out the subjugating presence of whiteness and the deleterious effects on identity that come from our often unwitting performance of whiteness.[21] "The white man is all around me;

---

[20]. W. E. B. Du Bois, *The Souls of Black Folk* (1903; New York: Dover Publications, 1994), 2.

[21]. It is widely recognized across many areas of research that identity categories such as gender, sexuality, and race are not merely ideological but also embodied realities. As such, one is not simply "white" or "Black"

up above the sky is tearing at its navel; the earth crunches under my feet and sings white, white. All this whiteness burns me to a cinder," declares Fanon.[22] What Fanon is highlighting is that white people generally do not see the way in which their comfort, their experience, and their cultural preferences dominate and shape all aspects of American life and therefore affect those who do not fit into such expectations of what counts as "normal."

In a 1963 address to schoolteachers, James Baldwin talked about how Black children recognize this dynamic of white normativity from the earliest ages.

> There is something else the Negro child can do, too. Every street boy—and I was a street boy, so I know—looking at the society which has produced him, looking at the standards of that society which are not honored by anybody, looking at your churches and the government and the politicians, understands that this structure is operated for someone else's benefit—not for his. And there's no room in it for him.[23]

Part of what it means to be white is to never have to think about what it means to be anything other than belonging in most

---

but *performs* that racial identity in a manner analogous to the performance of gender in everyday life. One analysis of the performance of whiteness in scholarly literature is found in John T. Warren, "Doing Whiteness: On the Performative Dimensions of Race in the Classroom," *Communication Education* 50 (April 2001): 91–108. See also Richard Delgado, *Critical Race Theory: The Cutting Edge*, 2nd ed. (Philadelphia: Temple University Press, 2000).

22. Frantz Fanon, *Black Skin, White Masks,* trans. Richard Philcox (New York: Grove Press, 2008), 94.

23. James Baldwin, "A Talk to Teachers," in *James Baldwin: Collected Essays*, ed. Toni Morrison (New York: Library of America, 1998), 681.

situations and places. This is something that I have come to see with greater and greater clarity over time, and it has helped me to reckon with the fact that we live in a white supremacist culture, which presumes my whiteness as the norm and those who look different from me as the exception or "other." Living in a racist society not only champions those aspects of my cultural formation and worldview, senses of beauty, and forms of comfort, but also makes clear that anything that does not reflect or conform to those standard norms is viewed and treated as inferior or worthless.

I have experienced this contrast growing up in a largely white community in Upstate New York where food preferences, aesthetic tastes, musical styles, clothing choices, and other forms of cultural expression that reflected the minority Black and Latinx populations of our city were regularly disparaged or at least viewed as "different" or "odd" by friends, family members, and strangers, usually unthinkingly. It wasn't until I had graduated from college and joined the Franciscan friars that I was not only exposed to but also immersed in cultures very different from my own—first in the South Bronx, then in the inner city of Wilmington, Delaware, then in a predominantly working-class Latinx community just outside Washington, DC, and then living for a summer in Bolivia. What was striking to me even at the time was not only how different everything seemed but also how long it took for me to realize and accept that these were wonderfully rich and equally dignified forms of cultural expression to what I had experienced in my upbringing. Because I presumed my white outlook, experiences, and cultural preferences were indeed "the norm," I found myself at first instinctively resistant and condescending in my internal assessment of what I encountered. It took a while for me to move beyond my initial discomfort and unfamiliarity with the references and habits I was being exposed to for the first time. The process not only allowed me to appreciate new perspectives and experiences—thanks to the patience, hospitality, and generosity of so many people of color—but also challenged me to rethink my own assumptions of white normativity and interrogate why I had felt so dismissive or uncomfortable when experiencing different cultures.

Scholars like Joe R. Feagin have described this phenomenon of whiteness being the primary lens through which whites and white institutions see the world as "the white racial frame."[24] Feagin explains that the white racial frame is "the dominant racial frame that has long legitimated, rationalized, motivated, and shaped racial oppression and inequality in this country. This white racial frame is a centuries-old worldview that has constantly involved a racial construction of societal reality by white Americans."[25] One common experience of what it means to be white in the United States is to (a) not see this operative framework governing everything from the green-lighting of new television sitcoms that are, as they have always been, predominantly white in cast and in culture to the establishment of policies and shaping of laws that disproportionately harm Blacks and other people of color; *and* (b) not generally be bothered by these same consequences that arise from the operative dynamics of the white racial frame. This is part of what is meant by "white privilege," which we'll explore in greater detail later in this book—namely, that to be white in America is to be typically unaffected in any negative way by the hegemonic presence of whiteness as the social and cultural norm in nearly all aspects of shared common life.

---

[24]. Joe R. Feagin, *The White Racial Frame: Centuries of Racial Framing and Counter-Framing*, 3rd ed. (New York: Routledge, 2020).

[25]. Feagin, *White Racial Frame*, 4.

Whiteness as Property

On the afternoon of February 23, 2020, in the suburban neighborhood of Brunswick, Georgia, a twenty-five-year-old Black man named Ahmaud Arbery went for a run. A former high-school athlete, Arbery ran regularly to keep healthy. Shortly after 1:00 p.m., Arbery ran by a sixty-four-year-old white man named Gregory McMichael standing in his front lawn, who called to his thirty-four-year-old son Travis McMichael, also a white man, to join him in pursuing Arbery. According to police reports, they were armed with a .357 magnum revolver and a shotgun.[26] Shortly thereafter they caught up with Arbery, who had continued his leisurely run and was unarmed. They called to him, a tussle ensued, and the two white men fatally shot Arbery out in the open of a public street on a Sunday afternoon.[27]

It took more than two months before an arrest was made. And then it was only due to the pressure officials in Georgia received from an outraged public that witnessed a viral video of the shooting, captured by a third white man, William "Roddie" Bryan, who was a neighbor of the McMichaels and was later also arrested for charges related to the killing of Arbery. On June 24, 2020—more than four months after Arbery's murder—a grand jury indicted all three white men on nine counts including malice murder, felony murder, aggravated assault, and false imprisonment. All three men were convicted of murder at trial.

[26.] Richard Fausset, "Two Weapons, a Chase, a Killing and No Charges," *New York Times*, April 26, 2020, https://www.nytimes.com/2020/04/26/us/ahmed-arbery-shooting-georgia.html.

[27.] Richard Fausset, "What We Know about the Shooting Death of Ahmaud Arbery," *New York Times*, June 24, 2020, https://www.nytimes.com/article/ahmaud-arbery-shooting-georgia.html.

Like millions of other people, I was horrified by this murder. It was not the first time that I had become aware of the widespread injustice experienced by people of color, but it hit me especially hard because of the particular circumstances of the case. Like Arbery, I am also a runner. Running is, without a doubt, the most consistent and rewarding hobby I have ever had. I love running, and it has been a big part of my life.

Whenever I travel to another place, I always run while I'm there. I have run in places where I have not always felt particularly comfortable because I am unfamiliar with the new location and because it is clear that I stick out. Such was the case when I spent a summer living with my brother Franciscan friars in Cochabamba, Bolivia, where both my height and my whiteness (and my commitment to running at an altitude of more than ten thousand feet above sea level) drew attention. I have run in rural North Carolina, where I was frightened to see Confederate flags flown off dilapidated porches, and I have run in the predawn morning of the roughest part of Philadelphia.

And though there were many other times when I was consciously uneasy with my surroundings or recognized that I was noticeably "out of place," I never feared that someone would deliberately shoot me because I looked "suspicious" to them (a loosely veiled racist euphemism to be sure). On some level, even when I was running through the wealthiest suburban white neighborhoods or running through Black neighborhoods afflicted with the worst of urban blight or running in another country where I did not speak the language well or at all, I somehow *knew* that at least the color of my skin would not affect me negatively, let alone make me a target for capricious murder. It is as if I had an innate sense of "my right" to run in each and every one of these vastly different places. It is as if my being white not only granted me a certain protection from undue harm but actually bestowed on me a kind of entitlement to be—and *to run*—wherever I please, whenever I please.

That what I recognize through my years of running is not limited to me alone but is the shared experience of all white people, whether admitted or not, is another part of what it means to be white in a racist society. It is not just that Ahmaud Arbery was Black and unfairly targeted and killed because of the color of his skin that reflects the injustice of our white supremacist and systemically racist society. It's that I as a white man, a white runner, also unwittingly *benefit* in concrete and identifiable ways from the very same social dynamics.[28]

In 1993 a legal scholar named Cheryl Harris published an important article in the *Harvard Law Review* in which she coined the phrase "whiteness as property" to name exactly the kind of phenomenon that I have come to recognize in my experiences of running, but that is always already operating in the everyday experiences of white people.[29] Harris painstakingly demonstrates how the legal system in the United States, from its very founding, established "whiteness" not only as a racial characteristic that distinguished some people from others in an arbitrary manner but also as a "traditional form of property" that bestowed on individuals categorized as white certain rights and privileges. Furthermore, these advantages were identified with the white individual such that they were always present as the personal property of the individual. Harris explains:

---

[28]. For more on this, see Daniel P. Horan, "Running While White," *National Catholic Reporter*, July 22, 2020.

[29]. Cheryl I. Harris, "Whiteness as Property," *Harvard Law Review* 106, no. 8 (1993): 1710–69. Reprinted in *Critical Race Theory: The Key Writings That Formed the Movement*, ed. Kimberlé Crenshaw, Neil Gotanda, Gary Peller, and Kendall Thomas (New York: New Press, 1995), 276–91. Further citations come from the anthology source.

> Whiteness defined the legal status of a person as slave or free. White identity conferred tangible and economically valuable benefits, and it was jealously guarded as a valued possession, allowed only to those who met a strict standard of proof. Whiteness—the right to white identity as embraced by the law—is property if by "property" one means all of a person's legal rights.[30]

As mentioned earlier, which communities counted as "white" shifted over time, further supporting the notion that whiteness is a property "jealously guarded as a valued possession" and only distributed to those selected. The consequences of being identified as white were and are manifold, resulting in unearned advantages—or, at the very least, the absence of additional burdens and obstacles that people of color must regularly confront.

Like other kinds of property, whiteness accrues value over a lifetime. This is what is commonly referred to as "white privilege"—those opportunities and advantages that are afforded to white people but denied to Black people and other people of color. The term can be somewhat misleading in that a commonsense understanding of "privilege" would seem to suggest that white people should be able to recognize some concrete benefits or at least not experience hardship. But life, particularly in a racist society such as the United States, is neither that simple nor that easy. We are more than just our race. We are also gendered and abled and intellectually variant, and we have a range of financial resources. This realization that identity and social context are the result of multiple, complex social and power disparities requires a form of analysis sometimes called "intersectionality," because to understand a *particular* person's

---

30. Harris, "Whiteness as Property," 280.

circumstances and social location requires analysis of all the *intersecting* social structures and dynamics that shape their experiences in the world. That said, within a racist society such as ours, one's perceived race plays a disproportionate role. One only has to think of examples such as that of former President Barack Obama or Harvard professor Henry Louis Gates Jr., both of whom are very successful and intelligent and powerful men, and yet both have also experienced discrimination and racist vitriol because they are *Black* men. Conversely, even the poorest, least educated, and otherwise socially disadvantaged white man will never have to endure the subtlest racial discrimination or the most overt racial animus on account of his race.

One of the simplest and most insightful illustrations of how white privilege functions in the United States was articulated by the gender-studies professor Peggy McIntosh in a now-classic article titled "White Privilege: Unpacking the Invisible Knapsack."[31] As a scholar of systemic oppression against women, whose own work included trying to get men to recognize the various ways their gender identity benefits them in large and small ways every day, it occurred to McIntosh at some point that a similar structural dynamic was at work in the way white people such as herself unwittingly benefited from unearned advantages in all sectors of life. She began to compile a list of conditions that she believed she benefited from on a daily basis because of "skin-color privilege" rather than on account of "class, religion, ethnic status, or geographical location."[32] She realized that Black women and men, including many of her

---

[31]. Peggy McIntosh, "White Privilege: Unpacking the Invisible Knapsack," in *White Privilege: Essential Readings on the Other Side of Racism*, ed. Paula S. Rothenberg, 5th ed. (New York: Macmillan, 2016), 151–55.

[32]. McIntosh, "White Privilege: Unpacking the Invisible Knapsack," 152.

equally qualified academic colleagues, could not count on these very same conditions, and she compiled a list of dozens of such circumstances and conditions. These include the following:

- I can if I wish arrange to be in the company of people of my race most of the time.
- If I should need to move, I can be pretty sure of renting or purchasing housing in an area which I can afford and in which I would want to live.
- I can be pretty sure that my neighbors in such a location will be neutral or pleasant to me.
- I can go shopping alone most of the time, pretty well assured that I will not be followed or harassed.
- I can turn on the television or open to the front page of the paper and see people of my race widely represented.
- When I am told about our national heritage or about "civilization," I am shown that people of my color made it what it is.
- I am never asked to speak for all the people of my racial group.
- I can be pretty sure that if I ask to talk to "the person in charge," I will be facing a person of my race.
- If a traffic cop pulls me over or if the IRS audits my tax return, I can be sure I haven't been singled out because of my race.
- I can easily buy posters, postcards, picture books, greeting cards, dolls, toys, and children's magazines featuring people of my race.
- I can choose blemish covers or bandages in "flesh" color and have them more or less match my skin.[33]

---

[33]. McIntosh, "White Privilege: Unpacking the Invisible Knapsack," 152–53. This is not an exhaustive list. In one version of this essay, McIntosh lists as many as fifty such conditions.

McIntosh's list unveils the subtlety of the "privileges" that come from whiteness as property in a racist and white supremacist society. But sometimes, as in the case of the contrast between my many experiences of running in nearly every sort of circumstance and location and the experience of Ahmaud Arbery, the implications of whiteness as property can be a matter of life and death.

To be a white person in the United States is to experience a kind of freedom from oppression that people of color are not granted. It is a form of benefiting from how power is distributed in all sectors of society, including in the Church and other Catholic organizations. This contrast was recently on display at the Jesuit Santa Clara University. In the summer of 2020, Danielle Fuentes Morgan, a Black woman and assistant professor of English, was called to her front door by the knocking of her brother. Carlos Fuentes, a music teacher from Sacramento, was in town to visit his sister and had stepped outside her university-subsidized faculty apartment to take a video work call outdoors in the beautiful California weather. At around 8:30 a.m., university security officers saw him, a Black man sitting on the idyllic campus with his laptop, and insisted that he "move along." He returned to his sister's apartment, followed by four university security officers. Upon their arrival, the officers demanded that Fuentes Morgan show her identification and "prove" that she lived in the apartment, the apartment she was *already standing inside* when they knocked! In an interview with the *Washington Post*, she said: "Being Black in America means there is an expectation that you have to show your papers, that you have to prove you are who you say you are and you belong where you say you belong."[34]

---

34. Teo Armus, "'I Wasn't Surprised. I Was Just Hurt': A Black Professor Says Campus Police Demanded Proof She Lives in Her Own

This is what it means to talk about the privilege and property of whiteness in American society, including in the Church and in Catholic institutions. People of color are routinely subjected to such humiliations and threats to their safety and lives. Meanwhile, white people rarely experience such harassment and are almost always presumed to be innocent or in the right by authorities. But because whiteness is socially constructed and not, strictly speaking, a "necessary" element of reality, it only exists as a result of the injustice of racism present in our communities. As Harris notes near the end of her article on whiteness as property, "Among whites, the idea persists that their whiteness is meaningful. Whiteness is an aspect of racial identity surely, but it is much more; it remains a concept based on relations of power, a social construct predicated on white dominance and black subordination."[35] For this reason, white people are reluctant to acknowledge that white privilege does in fact exist and, if they are able to accept this fundamental truth of our context, they are still reluctant to work to dismantle the systems that simultaneously advantage them and disadvantage people of color.

White Fragility and Rage

In the last chapter I described systemic racism in the United States as a "real conspiracy" that involves numerous factors coming together to harm certain communities of people (BIPOC) and advantage another (white people). The thing about conspiracies in general, at least when they are successful, is that they are not

---

House," *Washington Post*, August 24, 2020, https://www.washingtonpost.com/nation/2020/08/24/santa-clara-campus-police-professor/.

35. Harris, "Whiteness as Property," 287.

widely seen in the open. To pull off a conspiracy of any sort, it is useful to have a cloak of ignorance that covers over the truth of what is going on so that it can continue. Because of factors like whiteness as normative and the benefits afforded white people due to whiteness as property, many white folks generally live in a kind of blissful ignorance about how reality in a racist culture such as ours benefits them and harms others. But what happens when whites are confronted with the truth of racism and white privilege? Why is it that so many white people refuse to accept what so many Black people and other people of color have tried to communicate about systemic racism for years?

One reason that white people are frequently disinclined to confront the uncomfortable truths of racism and white privilege is because of what Robin DiAngelo has famously termed "white fragility."[36] DiAngelo, drawing on her decades-long work as an anti-racist activist and workshop facilitator, notes that it's frequently the case that when white people face the sorts of facts we have so far discussed in this book, they experience a range of intense emotional reactions. While the manifestation of these emotional reactions varies and can surface in ways like anger, sadness, withdrawal, argumentation, or something else, what is operating beneath the surface is a kind of defensiveness and denial. As DiAngelo summarizes, "White fragility is a state in which even a minimum amount of racial stress becomes intolerable, triggering a range of defensive moves."[37] She explains that there are various kinds of "triggers" that may set

---

[36]. Robin DiAngelo first developed this concept in an academic publication: "White Fragility," *International Journal of Critical Pedagogy* 3, no. 3 (2011): 54–70, and later expanded on the notion for a general audience in her book *White Fragility: Why It's So Hard for White People to Talk about Racism* (Boston: Beacon Books, 2018).

[37]. DiAngelo, *What Does It Mean to Be White?*, 247.

white people off, most of which are perceived by the triggered white person as "challenges" to the worldview they had long come to accept as true.

While some people may rightly feel that it is wrong to even talk about something like white fragility because it again places the comfort and experience of white people at the center of the discussion, I believe that DiAngelo's work in this area is especially useful in preparing for how we and other white people might respond when engaging in honest and challenging conversations about racism and privilege. Just as many white folks have gone out of their way to avoid confronting the real conspiracy operating in their midst and deny their own complicity in it, many others take a more active role in the perpetuation of systemic racism and maintenance of white privilege by not holding other white people accountable through respectful but direct dialogue. Given the widespread belief among whites that "racism" is only ever about morally reprehensible *individuals* doing abhorrent and inexcusable *actions* toward people of color, what Massingale calls "commonsense racism," the fact that they might be challenged to see their own racism and participation in a racist society is too much for them to handle. This is not an excuse or justification to remain willfully ignorant about racism, but it is an important insight as to why such unjust systems, structures, institutions, attitudes, and perspectives persist, especially among white people.

There is a sort of ironic cycle that many white people trap themselves in on account of white fragility. The fear of being called a "racist" or called out for saying or doing something perceived as racially insensitive preemptively shuts down many attempts to say anything about race at all. I know that I have experienced this sort of fear, which DiAngelo would note is symptomatic of white fragility. The self-consciousness that arises within me for fear of "saying the wrong thing" or unwittingly revealing my internalized racism has, on sadly too many occasions, motivated both my silence and my defensiveness. The silence comes when I should have said something while witnessing racist comments, jokes, or behaviors. The silence also appears when I should have asked about the experiences of people of color or respectfully inquired about something that was confusing or unclear to me, but I didn't speak up because I was embarrassed for not knowing already or because I was fearful that I would offend my dialogue partner by saying the wrong thing. The silence is also present too often when people close to me—friends, colleagues, or family members—say or do something that I know is inaccurate or even overtly racist, but I just "let it go" because I am concerned about rocking the boat of our relationship. In all these cases, it is white fragility and comfort—mine and that of others—that I have prioritized over what is right and just.

But silence is not the only problematic response that emerges from the condition of unacknowledged white fragility. On those occasions when I have spoken out or asked a question or made a comment or joke that was perceived by a person of color as racist, I have gotten defensive. I know from my own experiences how easy it is for white people to assume that the internal good intentions we operate with should justify what we say or do. I recall one time when I was attempting to compliment a friend of mine for his particularly fastidious and organized interior design style. I was grasping for a way to articulate to a third person in the conversation what I liked about this friend's distinctive style. I said something along the lines of his style reflecting a kind of feng shui aesthetic, with everything located in what always struck me as a simple yet harmonious layout. My friend, who is Filipino, became agitated and asked rhetorically why so many people say this kind of thing when he is not Chinese. I could tell he was upset, but I was confused and unsure of what I had done wrong.

To me, I considered the "feng shui" descriptor an innocuous remark intending to be a compliment, something that I believed I would have said to anybody with such an aesthetic style resembling my friend's preferences. It did not occur to me that the cultural origin of the style movement being Chinese would understandably trigger a person of Asian descent who was not Chinese, given that he clearly encountered racist stereotypes about the homogeneity of Asian culture and identity. I was only ever familiar with the typical American reference to a pop-culture phenomenon in the 1990s that, to me, did not describe a particular Asian culture or identity but a general sense of interior decorating style. I could tell he was upset, I could tell that I had said something wrong, but my internal defensiveness led me to justify—at least to myself—that what I said was perfectly acceptable because I meant no harm. Clearly, I wasn't being racist; I was only trying to compliment my friend, who had the nerve to misinterpret my gesture of generosity. But what I didn't consider at the time was that maybe his frustration was entirely merited. In the moment and immediately afterward I only considered my intention and not how, as St. Thomas Aquinas would put it, what I said was received in the mode of the receiver. I wasn't attentive to the way in which his life experience, his worldview, and his race contributed to receiving what I said in a way that was hurtful or triggering. In other words, intention is not enough, and my white fragility led me to embrace a defensive stance rather than a position open to learning and growing.

While most white Americans resist talking about or acknowledging the uncomfortable realities of racism and privilege and often act in accord with some kind of white fragility, others are far more explicitly defensive and hostile in their response. The historian Carol Anderson has written about what she calls "white rage" to help identify some of what is going on, generally beneath the surface, in the perpetuation of systemic racism and white privilege in the American context.[38] Whereas "white fragility" might helpfully diagnose the reticence of most whites to confront their own complicity in systems and cultures of racial injustice, "white rage" is used to describe the recurring backlash from whites to "every action of African American advancement."[39]

As people of color know all too well, the history of the United States is not as praiseworthy or oriented toward progress as most white Americans would like to believe or frequently recount in their telling. Anderson provides in painstaking detail how after each seeming advance toward racial justice in the United States, a backlash—usually in legislative form—arises to bolster the system of racist suppression. Anderson explains that "white rage carries an aura of respectability and has access to the courts, police, legislatures and governors, who cast its efforts as noble, though they are actually driven by the most ignoble motivations."[40] It's easy for powerful whites on television and in the halls of governmental power to decry so-called violence and

---

[38]. Carol Anderson, *White Rage: The Unspoken Truth of Our Racial Divide* (London: Bloomsbury, 2016).

[39]. Carol Anderson, "Ferguson Isn't about Black Rage against Cops. It's White Rage against Progress," *Washington Post*, August 29, 2014, https://www.washingtonpost.com/opinions/ferguson-wasnt-black-rage-against-copsit-was-white-rage-against-progress/2014/08/29/3055e3f4-2d75-11e4-bb9b-997ae96fad33_story.html.

[40]. Anderson, "Ferguson Isn't about Black Rage against Cops. It's White Rage against Progress."

riots associated with the Black community's efforts to protest sustained, systemic oppression. Oftentimes one hears these white leaders call for "law and order" or some other euphemism that seeks to delegitimize the righteous grievance of the people protesting. We have seen this in recent years: in 2014 in Ferguson, Missouri, after the killing of Michael Brown; in 2015 in Baltimore, Maryland, after the killing of Freddie Gray; and in 2020 all around the world after the killing of George Floyd. Each murder of an unarmed Black man set off the righteous anger of a people who have never experienced real justice in the American context, and the response of those whites in power is to denounce ancillary violence or looting, shifting the focus away from the uncomfortable truths about our society and institutions in order to blame the victim yet again.

I am reminded of something the Catholic priest and Trappist monk Thomas Merton wrote in the 1960s, which illustrates well exactly what Anderson means by the white rage that is operating beneath the surface in the face of the anguished cries for justice. Merton observed:

> But it must be remembered that the crime that breaks out of the ghetto is only the fruit of a greater and more pervasive violence: the injustice which forces people to live in the ghetto in the first place. The problem of violence, then, is not the problem of a few rioters and rebels, *but the problem of a whole social structure which is outwardly ordered and respectable, and inwardly ridden by psychopathic obsessions and delusions.*[41]

---

[41]. Thomas Merton, "Toward a Theology of Resistance," in *Faith and Violence* (Notre Dame, IN: University of Notre Dame Press, 1968), 3, emphasis added.

What Merton describes here is what Anderson names as the unacknowledged white rage that simmers beneath a racist façade of "order" and "respectability." Nothing will change until white people are willing to overcome the lies they have long believed and face the hard truths few have been willing to address.

As true as white fragility and rage are in the broader society, so too are they realities in our Church. While the Catholic Church in the American context is becoming increasingly diversified in terms of demographics, reflecting more the composition of the Global South than that of Europe, the vast majority of priests and bishops here are still white. The dynamics and history DiAngelo and Anderson help illuminate give us insight into why so few preachers ever mention racism or white privilege in their homilies and why so few parishes offer workshops or other programming that addresses these topics head-on. As we will see in greater detail later, in chapter 5, these insights also help to explain why the documents on race and racial justice published by the United States Conference of Catholic Bishops (USCCB) are often so inadequate. Just as white people will not address the painful realities of racism in their homes, workplaces, and society more broadly, so too white Catholics are reluctant (or even hostile) to name, acknowledge, and address these subjects in the Church.

Further Reading

- Robert P. Amico, *Exploring White Privilege* (New York: Routledge, 2017).
- Carol Anderson, *White Rage: The Unspoken Truth of Our Racial Divide* (London: Bloomsbury, 2016).
- Robin DiAngelo, *What Does It Mean to Be White? Developing White Racial Literacy*, rev. ed. (New York: Peter Lang, 2016).

- Robin DiAngelo, *White Fragility: Why It's So Hard for White People to Talk about Racism* (Boston: Beacon Press, 2018).
- Kelly Brown Douglas, *Stand Your Ground: Black Bodies and the Justice of God* (Maryknoll, NY: Orbis Books, 2015).
- Frantz Fanon, *Black Skin, White Masks*, trans. Richard Philcox (New York: Grove Press, 2008).
- Joe R. Feagin, *The White Racial Frame: Centuries of Racial Framing and Counter-Framing*, 3rd ed. (New York: Routledge, 2020).
- Robert Jenson, *The Heart of Whiteness: Confronting Race, Racism, and White Privilege* (San Francisco: City Lights Books, 2005).
- Nell Irvin Painter, *The History of White People* (New York: W. W. Norton, 2010).
- Paula S. Rothenberg, ed., *White Privilege: Essential Readings on the Other Side of Racism*, 5th ed. (New York: Macmillan, 2016).
- Tim Wise, *White Like Me: Reflections on Race from a Privileged Son*, rev. ed. (Berkeley, CA: Soft Skull Press, 2011).
- George Yancy, *Look, a White! Philosophical Essays on Whiteness* (Philadelphia: Temple University Press, 2012).

3

Racism Is a White Problem

There are few people who have captured the tragedy and complexity of America's racist reality—past and present—with as much eloquence as the writer James Baldwin. Writing primarily in the middle of the twentieth century, he courageously wrote and spoke the truth that white people were reluctant to hear and that Black people were understandably tired of trying to explain. In 1965 Baldwin wrote an article titled "The White Man's Guilt," which opens with the powerful inquiry: "I have often wondered, and it is not a pleasant wonder, just what white Americans talk about with one another."[1] The implication at the outset of his essay is that there must be some kind of fantastical narrative and code that white people tell themselves to allow them to remain inert in the face of the tremendous oppression and injustice for which white people are wholly responsible. Baldwin surmises that whatever they feel comfortable communicating to him as a Black man is not the whole picture. He explains:

> And what they see is an appallingly oppressive and bloody history, known all over the world. What they see is a disastrous, continuing, present, condition which

---

[1]. James Baldwin, "The White Man's Guilt," in *James Baldwin: Collected Essays*, ed. Toni Morrison (New York: Library of America, 1998), 722.

menaces them, and for which they bear an inescapable responsibility. But since, in the main, they seem to lack the energy to change this condition, they would rather not be reminded of it. Does this mean that, in their conversations with one another, they merely make reassuring sounds? It scarcely seems possible, and yet, on the other hand, it seems all too likely. In any case, whatever they bring to one another, it is certainly not freedom from guilt. The guilt remains, more deeply rooted, more securely lodged, than the oldest of old trees.[2]

In some sense what Baldwin is naming and diagnosing is what is operating beneath the surface of the experience and thoughts of most white people in a racist society. This sense of "guilt" Baldwin names is likely not conscious in the minds of most whites, but nevertheless remains always already present in our hearts. It is triggered when confronted with the inescapable truths about racism and white privilege, and the typical response by whites is fragility and rage.

Baldwin here and elsewhere throughout his volumes of magnificent prose speaks of the truth that haunts white people: racism is a *white problem*. The personal and collective guilt white people try to suppress and ignore originates from the historical fact that a racist culture and society, systems of inequality and oppression, and the establishment and maintenance of institutions of slavery are not mere coincidences or natural occurrences. Racism in the United States is the result of the deliberate choices enacted by white people over the course of centuries, and it continues to this day. Systemic racism and the white privilege that accompanies it are not accidental but

---

[2]. Baldwin, "The White Man's Guilt," 722.

intentional, and the historical record bears this out. Baldwin writes: "One wishes that Americans, white Americans, would read, for their own sakes, this record, and stop defending themselves against it. Only then will they be enabled to change their lives."[3]

Returning to Baldwin's question about what white people say to one another, the uncomfortable truth is that white people in big and little, overt and covert ways perpetuate the lies and myths that ameliorate the burden of the justified guilt that we carry within us. It is a historical guilt, it is a collective guilt, and it is also a personal guilt. Guilt, particularly within a Catholic context, is not merely pathological or a joke but can be a useful factor in identifying sin and wrongdoing. Guilt, like the sharp feeling of pain upon touching a hot stove, can serve to signal to our consciousness what our consciences register as sinful and in need of repentance and reconciliation. But guilt for its own sake is worthless. There is no good in feeling bad for the sake of feeling bad. The good of guilt comes only in guilt leading to contrition, repentance, and restorative action.

In the two previous chapters we explored what racism and whiteness actually mean, helping to uncover the often-overlooked complexities of racism and race. This chapter continues the work of unpacking the significance of these realities that white people have long dismissed or ignored. Because racism is a white problem, it requires work and transformation on the part of white people. This begins with a willingness to sit with the discomfort and to acknowledge the pain that systemic racism and white privilege have wrought. It continues with attuning oneself to the manifold ways cultural racism is always already operative in our communities and institutions, as well as in our

---

[3]. Baldwin, "The White Man's Guilt," 722.

personal and shared assumptions, perceptions, and judgments. In what follows, we will look at why it seems as if nothing ever changes in terms of racial justice; examine the role of white power; consider how popular culture, media, and society factor into perpetuating racism; and look at how white people in particular are socialized into a white supremacist worldview that, among other things, contributes to the formation of implicit bias.

Why Doesn't Anything Seem to Change?

There are a lot of intersecting factors that contribute to the persistence of racial injustice in our society and Church. But given the primary audience of this book and my own experience and perspective as a white man concerned about addressing systemic racism and white privilege, I want to focus on one major impediment to change in the work for racial justice. The honest and painful truth is that things have not and seemingly will not change because *white people don't want things to change.*

Some of you reading this will likely feel the urge to get defensive and begin listing all the ways in which my claim that, generally speaking, white people do not want our white supremacist society to change does not reflect your personal views and commitments. On the one hand, I completely understand where you're coming from (I am also a white person, after all). On the other hand, this is one of those moments I described early in this book that would be necessarily uncomfortable for many white people.

As Fr. Bryan Massingale put it bluntly in a 2020 interview with *Commonweal* magazine, "The only reason for the persistence of racism is because white people benefit from it."[4]

---

4. Regina Munch, "'Worship of a False God': An Interview with Bryan Massingale," *Commonweal*, June 5, 2020, https://www.commonwealmagazine.org/worship-false-god.

This statement arose within the context of his explaining how conversations about racism and racial justice, particularly in the Catholic Church but also more broadly, are often dictated by the threshold of white comfort. In response to questions from well-meaning white people who become aware of the realities of systemic racism and white privilege and who ask about what they can do in turn, Massingale says the following:

> I challenge them to think of this: if it were up to people of color, racism would have been over and done, resolved a long time ago. The only reason that racism continues to persist is because white people benefit from it. If we're always going to have conversations that are predicated upon preserving white comfort, then we will never get beyond the terrible impasse that we're in, and we will always doom ourselves to superficial words and to ineffective half-measures. That difficult truth is something that the Catholic Church in America has never summoned the courage or the will to directly address.[5]

More than a half century earlier, James Baldwin described the same dynamic at work—the willful ignorance and desire to maintain a plausible deniability among white folks. Referring to the horrendous record of anti-Black racist attacks during the civil rights era in the American South, Baldwin summarized his sense of white denial about what they were forced to confront through their television screens and newspaper pages. He wrote: "White people are astounded by Birmingham. Black people aren't. White people are endlessly demanding to be reassured that Birmingham is really on Mars." And in an effort to demonstrate how pervasive

---

5. Munch, "'Worship of a False God': An Interview with Bryan Massingale."

systemic racism is in America and not simply located in the "racist South," he added that white people "don't want to believe, still less act on the belief, that what is happening in Birmingham . . . is happening all over the country, and has been for countless generations; they don't want to realize that there is not one step, one inch, no distance, morally or actually, between Birmingham and Los Angeles."[6]

Despite occasional and often long-overdue court decisions and legislation that attempt to address racial injustices, little in practice changes.[7] The biggest factor is not often-unapologetic racists whose unhidden white supremacist ideology somehow afflicts millions of people of color, but the indifference, complacency, and silence of white people. White people invented racism. White people built a nation on the backs of Indigenous genocide and an economy based on chattel slavery. White people fought a bloody Civil War to defend the self-appointed "right" to own other human beings and profit from their wealth. White people rolled back any meager attempt at civil rectitude during the postwar Reconstruction era by passing the horrifying laws and practices of the Jim Crow era. White people, threatened by the peaceful and righteous cause of the civil rights movement, hated Martin Luther King Jr. during his life and recast his legacy as unthreatening and milquetoast after his murder.[8] White people, who disproportionately hold

---

6. James Baldwin, "The White Problem," in *The Cross of Redemption: Uncollected Writings*, ed. Randall Kenan (New York: Vintage Books, 2011), 96–97.

7. For instance, see Richard Rothstein, *The Color of Law: A Forgotten History of How Our Government Segregated America* (New York: W. W. Norton, 2017).

8. For another look at the speeches and positions of Martin Luther King Jr., see *The Radical King*, ed. Cornel West (Boston: Beacon Press,

political office and power, led the charge to pass legislation that disproportionately criminalizes and incarcerates people of color.[9]

White people, threatened by the truth of their complicity in the structures of injustice that lead to police murdering unarmed Black women and men time and again, find themselves unbearably triggered by the righteous cry that "Black Lives Matter" and respond with a racist slogan that is as deluded as it is intended to be diluting, "all lives matter." Many white people do not immediately recognize why saying "all lives matter" in this context is racist. At first glance, it would appear to be an inclusive statement. However, the expression "Black Lives Matter" is invoked to draw attention to the fact that in the United States our laws, customs, and institutions do not actually treat the lives and bodies of Black women, men, and children as if they did matter. It points out a painful truth—a truth about the omission of justice, a truth about the inequity of our communities. To respond with "all lives matter" is to deliberately or unwittingly deny or reject the basic fact of systemic racism, to claim an ideal of justice that is not real in practice. Tragically, some whites invoke "all lives matter" to insist that they are somehow the actual victims.

Baldwin wasn't the only one attuned to the "signs of the times," as painful and discomfiting as they were in the 1960s and remain today. Thomas Merton wrote a lengthy essay in

---

2015); James Cone, *Martin & Malcolm & America: A Dream or a Nightmare* (Maryknoll, NY: Orbis Books, 2012); and Anthony E. Cook, "Beyond Critical Legal Studies: The Reconstructive Theology of Dr. Martin Luther King, Jr.," in *Critical Race Theory: The Key Writings That Formed the Movement*, ed. Kimberlé Crenshaw, Neil Gotanda, Gary Peller, and Kendall Thomas (New York: New Press, 1995), 85–102.

9. Michelle Alexander, *The New Jim Crow: Mass Incarceration in the Age of Colorblindness* (New York: New Press, 2010).

response to Martin Luther King Jr.'s now-famous "Letter from Birmingham Jail." In it he reflected on the significance of the nonviolent protests for racial justice led by King and others, and he concluded correctly what the purpose of the civil rights movement was and *who* it justly indicted:

> The purpose of non-violent protest, in its deepest and most spiritual dimensions is then to awaken the conscience of the white man to the awful reality of his injustice and of his sin, so that he will be able to see that the Negro problem is really a *White* problem: that the cancer of injustice and hate which is eating white society and is only partly manifested in racial segregation with all its consequences, *is rooted in the heart of the white man himself.*[10]

Like Baldwin, Merton is correct. Racism is a white problem. Indeed, nothing will change until white people come to this realization that they—*we*—are the problem and, therefore, we are responsible for working toward a solution.

In his 1964 essay, Baldwin speaks about the possibility of change and the unlikely chance that white people will do anything about it.

> I prefer to believe that since a society is created by men, it can be remade by men. The price of this transformation is high. White people will have to ask themselves precisely why they found it necessary to invent the n****r; for the

---

[10] Thomas Merton, "Letters to a White Liberal," in *Seeds of Destruction* (New York: Farrar, Straus, and Giroux, 1964), 45–46, emphasis original.

n****r is a white invention, and white people invented him out of terrible necessities of their own. And every white citizen of this country will have to accept the fact that he is not innocent, because those dogs and those hoses are being turned on American children, on American soil, with the tacit consent of the American Republic; those crimes are being committed in your name. Black people will have to do something very hard, too, which is to allow the white citizen his first awkward steps toward maturity.[11]

In Merton's attempts to understand, as a white man and a Catholic monk, what King and Baldwin and others were telling their white sisters and brothers, he recognized not only that racism is a white problem but that any real hope is rooted in the conversion of white people to see the change they must become. He wrote: "We must dare to pay the dolorous price of change, *to grow into a new society*. Nothing else will suffice! The only way out of this fantastic impasse is for everyone to face and accept the difficulties and sacrifices involved, in all their seriousness, in all their inexorable demands."[12]

The question is not, *Who did it?* or *Whose fault is it?* The question is, *What are you and I going to do about it?* Are we responsible to do something about it? Are we able to, as Merton urged, "accept the difficulties and sacrifices involved" in working toward real racial justice? Or are we going to continue to shield ourselves from the righteous cries of our sisters and brothers seeking justice?

---

[11]. Baldwin, "The White Problem," 97. [Author note: I have censored the use of the n-word in this quote.]

[12]. Merton, "Letters to a White Liberal," 9, emphasis in original.

The Role of White Power

Power is oftentimes understood in overly simplified terms, much like the way racism is often misunderstood. For many people, the notion of power has to do with the ability to exercise force against another. We might think of this as something like a "superhero power," as some kind of ability to directly help or harm another through sheer strength. This sense of power is also regularly used to describe the dynamics of difference between those in authority and those under authority. Teachers have the "power" to grade an assignment or send a student to detention; police officers have the "power" to detain and arrest someone; and employers have the "power" to hire and fire workers. In each of these commonplace examples, power is that which an individual or group of individuals holds over and against others. So when we talk about an entire category of people—white people in America, for example—as having and benefiting from "power" afforded to them by their whiteness, it strikes many white people as incomprehensible at best and absurd at worst. This is often the case because many white people do not actively *feel* like we wield power over others.

But power rarely functions in the real world in such a clear unilateral and unidirectional manner. Yes, it is fair to say that teachers and police officers and employers "have power" over others within their professional capacities and when they are exercising their respective socially prescribed offices. However, power is often a more diffuse and subtle reality, one that everyone participates in like the air we breathe or the time and space we inhabit. It can be difficult to recognize who has what power, particularly if you are the one who inhabits a position of power that you yourself are unable to see.

This is something that I have had to confront a lot in my own life. I am a cisgender man (which means that my gender identity aligns with the biological sex I was assigned at birth), an ordained Catholic priest, a member of a large and internationally respected religious order, a professor of theology and spirituality, an author and speaker recognized for my work around the world, a columnist at a national newspaper, an able-bodied person with generally good health, a neurotypical person (meaning I am not classified as having cognitive, mood, or social disabilities), and someone who is a documented citizen of the United States. And, of course, *I am white*. All of these characteristics, which partially describe what is referred to as my "social location," help give language to the tremendous amount of unearned power from which I benefit. I am almost always treated with respect and taken seriously, my presence is not treated with suspicion, nor am I typically made to feel uncomfortable because of my mere presence in a location. There are few places in the world where I don't easily feel comfortable and generally welcome. That is a very nice feeling. And because it is my usual experience, it can shield me from the fact that this is not how most other people—most women, people of color, transgender persons, laity, lower-educated people, disabled people, undocumented immigrants, and others—experience the world. If I do not step back to see how I fit into a much larger social landscape, I can easily slip into assuming that my experience is universal and the norm for everyone else, which it most certainly is not.

But what that familiarity and sense of normativity also do is blind me to the immense amount of power that I unwittingly wield in this society. When I am pulled over by the police for driving too fast on the highway (embarrassingly, something I have experienced . . . more than once), I have never had to fear for my physical safety. It never occurred to me that the police officer, regardless of that person's race or gender, would shoot me in the course of what I experienced as a routine traffic stop. The worst-case scenario for me was the hassle of a speeding ticket. When I am in meetings, whether in fancy boardrooms as a trustee of a university or at an academic conference or as a consultant in another context, I have always been listened to with respect and attention, never dismissed outright or talked over, and oftentimes treated with presumed deference. When I speak, people listen. When I complain, action follows. When I am present, I am taken seriously.

It has taken me a long time to realize that this is not the case for many, many people—that my experience is not at all normative, but exceptional. I am automatically bestowed authority. That power imbalance, particularly as it relates to the ways that race factors in a racist society, can be more than a little consequential; it could cost someone their life.

One of the more public illustrations of this racial power imbalance took place in Central Park in New York City on Memorial Day in 2020. A Black man named Christian Cooper, an avid bird-watcher, was in the park spotting various bird species as he often did on a daily basis, when he happened upon a dog off a leash in a part of the park that explicitly required dogs to be leashed, an ordinance designed in part to preserve the birds' habitat. The *Washington Post* reported that "around 7:30 a.m., he [Christian Cooper] spotted a rowdy, 2-year-old Henry [dog] grazing through the brush, as his owner, an investment manager in leggings and a face mask, was standing right by a sign saying all dogs must be leashed."[13]

---

13. Teo Armus, "White Woman 'Terminated' from Job after Calling Police on Black Birdwatcher Who Asked Her to Leash Her

Christian Cooper asked the woman to comply with the posted signs about leashing dogs, and she refused. The woman, Amy Cooper (no relation to the man with the same last name), was white and indignant that someone—a Black man—would insist that she abide by the laws of the city and park. Christian Cooper began filming the encounter on his phone, the video later went viral, and what it captures is a white woman threatening to deploy the power her whiteness bestowed on her against a Black man whose only "crime" was to respectfully request that this white woman *actually follow the law*. She threatened to call the cops, an unnecessary action that Christian Cooper nevertheless calmly encouraged her to do if she wanted, and she said, "And I'm going to tell them that there's an African American man threatening my life." Notice the escalation. Notice who is threatening whom. As he remained calm, she continued to work herself up into a furor and dialed 911. On the call, she spoke and screamed as if under attack or facing imminent threat of physical violence.

The video, which is easily accessible online, is not pleasant to view. Fortunately, nobody was physically harmed, but Amy Cooper's sense of white entitlement and her threat and deployment of white power against an innocent, law-abiding Black man who merely wished to bird-watch and have his safety and the safety of the animals in the park abided, put Christian Cooper's life in jeopardy. Reflecting on the incident in a powerful essay in *National Catholic Reporter*, Bryan Massingale lists the assumptions and privileges operating in the thoughts, words, and actions of Amy Cooper and her use of white power in the video. These include the following:

Dog, Company Says," *Washington Post*, May 27, 2020, https://www.washingtonpost.com/nation/2020/05/26/amy-cooper-central-park/.

- She assumed that her lies would be more credible than his truth.
- She assumed that she would have the presumption of innocence.
- She assumed that he, the black man, would have a presumption of guilt.
- She assumed that the police would back her up.
- She assumed that her race would be an advantage—that she would be believed because she is white. (By the way, this is what we mean by white privilege.)
- She assumed that his race would be a burden, even an insurmountable one.
- She assumed that the world should work for her and against him.
- She assumed that she had the upper hand in this situation.
- She assumed that she could exploit deeply ingrained white fears of black men.
- She assumed that she could use these deeply ingrained white fears to keep a black man in his place.
- She assumed that if he protested his innocence against her, he would be seen as "playing the race card."
- She assumed that no one would accuse her of "playing the race card," because no one accuses white people of playing the race card when using race to their advantage.
- She assumed that he knew that any confrontation with the police would not go well for him.
- She assumed that the frame of "black rapist" versus "white damsel in distress" would be clearly understood by everyone: the police, the press and the public.
- She assumed that the racial formation of white people would work in her favor.
- She assumed that her knowledge of how white people view the world, and especially black men, would help her.

- She assumed that a black man had no right to tell her what to do.
- She assumed that the police officers would agree.
- She assumed that even if the police made no arrest, that a lot of white people would take her side and believe her anyway.
- She assumed that Christian Cooper could and would understand all of the above.[14]

This haunting list displays her assumed power over him, and it is disturbing, not because it is exceptional and limited to a fluke circumstance in this particular park and on this particular morning but because it is *not exceptional* at all. White people *normally* and often unconsciously presume such power.

Later in statements and interviews with Amy Cooper, who lost her job once her employer learned of her overtly racist behavior captured on video, she explained that she was not totally aware of what she was doing at the time. She went into a kind of "automatic pilot" mode. And I believe her. That's the danger and insidiousness of the power that whiteness bestows on those perceived as white in a racist society. This is why it is absolutely necessary that white women and men learn to recognize and acknowledge the reality of this power imbalance and the ways whites have been socialized to consciously and unconsciously depend on it. When it rears its ugly head, manifestations of white power such as displayed in the Amy Cooper case could result in a death sentence for another innocent person of color.

If you think this is hyperbole, spend some time learning about the long-standing history of white women's lies and

---

14. Bryan N. Massingale, "The Assumptions of White Privilege and What We Can Do about It," *National Catholic Reporter*, June 1, 2020, https://www.ncronline.org/news/opinion/assumptions-white-privilege-and-what-we-can-do-about-it.

threats, not unlike those of Amy Cooper recorded on video, that have directly caused the lynching and murder of innocent Black men and boys.[15] Perhaps the most widely known instance is that of the gruesome murder of Emmett Till, a fourteen-year-old boy in Mississippi, who was accused of whistling at a white woman.[16] Sadly and disturbingly, the occasions of deployment of such white power against people of color are too long a list to catalog here. Without us white folks doing the difficult work of uncovering and confronting this power imbalance in our own lives, we remain complicit in the perpetuation of its deployment against others. And without the critical reflection necessary in advance, we may very well find ourselves in Amy Cooper's shoes someday—and the result might be far graver than we can imagine in the moment. It might cost someone else their life.

Popular Culture, Media, Society

You may be thinking to yourself: *But where does someone like Amy Cooper learn to rely on the unspoken assumptions that Massingale identified?* It's often said that nobody is born racist, and I believe that is true. However, *everybody* born in the United States *is born into a racist society* that shapes identity, perception, and action from the very beginning. One of the ways that a common

---

[15]. For a powerful testament to the horrendous history of chattel slavery, Jim Crow subjugation, segregation, and the persistence of Black lynchings in the United States, see the resources made available at the Legacy Museum in Montgomery, Alabama, https://museumandmemorial.eji.org/museum.

[16]. Library of Congress, "The Murder of Emmett Till," Civil Rights History Project, accessed February 1, 2021, https://www.loc.gov/collections/civil-rights-history-project/articles-and-essays/murder-of-emmett-till/.

perspective and outlook is formed and maintained is through popular culture and forms of entertainment. In many ways, the entertainment industry—including movies, television, music, books, art, internet memes, and so on—has a greater impact and longer efficacy in shaping opinions and outlooks than more traditional modes of education, such as the kind one receives in a high-school classroom. The creative arts that give us emotionally evocative music and fantastical fiction in books and film also reinscribe certain assumptions and perspectives that, because of their broad reach and hegemonic presence in a given society, are deeply significant. This is particularly true when depictions of people or communities, cultures or perspectives, unlike one's own are portrayed in popular culture and media in a negative light (or no light at all, making whole groups and perspectives invisible). And if you are a young white person in a community of predominantly white people and the only time you see people of color is on television, how they are portrayed will inform your own assumptions and views. The same is true about the way you think of whiteness, which is equally communicated throughout society by popular culture and media—generally speaking, whiteness is never named, but always presented and reinforced as invisible and normative.

What I am talking about here is the formation of what sociologist Joe Feagin calls "the white racial frame," which we looked at briefly in the last chapter when examining whiteness as normative.[17] When we ask questions like, "How does a white person learn these negative stereotypes about people of color?" or, "Where do these recurring stereotypes about Black people come from?" we are really asking about the formation of

---

17. Joe R. Feagin, *The White Racial Frame: Centuries of Racial Framing and Counter-Framing*, 3rd ed. (New York: Routledge, 2020).

a white way of viewing the world and of narrating reality. Feagin outlines the complex realities that, overtly and tacitly, conspire together to form the white racial frame as the normative lens through which our society is viewed and evaluated. It begins with the disingenuous manner in which our history is narrated, the way that those in power—white people—water down the horrors of genocide and enslavement, or frequently sidestep the persistence of racial injustice at each stage of our national memory. He writes about the "collective memories and collective forgetting" that enshrine certain depictions of the past and present, almost exclusively conditioned by an unspoken desire to maintain white people's comfort and avoid triggering what Robin DiAngelo calls "white fragility." This white racial frame, this sense of whiteness as normative, governs presumptions across society, including in politics, legislation, natural- and social-scientific research, medicine, theology, and every other aspect of our shared existence in the American context.[18] This was certainly my experience throughout my schooling and into adulthood, and it affected my way of understanding the world through the lens of white normativity. These instances when the white racial frame is operative are oftentimes subtle and difficult to recognize, but one major area of consistent and, generally speaking, more overt reinscription of the white racial frame is the entertainment industry.

Tracing this line of influence back to the nineteenth and twentieth centuries, Feagin notes: "Perhaps more important than the print media in spreading major aspects of the white racial frame were various forms of popular entertainment, especially minstrel shows and, later, vaudeville shows."[19] What makes these examples so striking is the explicitness with which

---

[18.] Feagin, *White Racial Frame*, 10–33.
[19.] Feagin, *White Racial Frame*, 84.

white people represent to other white people harmful depictions of Black people through performances by white entertainers wearing "blackface." Feagin explains:

> Again we observe the centuries-old white obsession with black Americans. White minstrel shows proclaimed racist epithets, mocked black English dialects, and offered white men fantasies of oversexed black men and women. Black men were mocked vigorously as "Zip Coon" dandies, and black women were stereotyped as sexualized and promiscuous. Racist "Aunt Jemima" mammy imagery originally surfaced in minstrel shows, later becoming widely circulated on U.S. commercial products. The shows also accented the supposed virtuousness of whites and "white civilization," drawing on and reinforcing the center of the dominant white racial frame. The performances celebrated whiteness by indicating that the audience members, a majority usually white workers, were not like the "darkies" negatively portrayed on stage. Minstrelsy was a critical way that key visual images, stereotypes, emotions, and interpretive understandings of the white racist framing were spread, especially to illiterate whites, new white immigrants, and younger whites.[20]

While this form of racist entertainment dominated the market in the nineteenth and early twentieth centuries, the advent of other entertainment media in the twentieth century—such as

---

[20]. Feagin, *White Racial Frame*, 85. See also Eric Lott, *Love and Theft: Blackface Minstrelsy and the American Working Class* (New York: Oxford University Press, 1993); and M. M. Manring, *Slave in a Box: The Strange Career of Aunt Jemima* (Charlottesville: University Press of Virginia, 1998).

radio, motion pictures, and television—did not mitigate the persistence and reinforcement of this deleterious construction of what it meant to be Black and what it meant to be white (namely, "not-Black") according to the white racial frame. One only has to think about who represents which communities of people on TV and the "big screen" and, even more importantly, *how* such people are represented. Massingale recounts in his book an internet posting from a blogger on CNN, who writes: "As a white male in a white state who has seen more black people on [the television show] *COPS* than in real life, I have to say it does feel odd sometimes that I'm supporting Obama with every ounce of my being. . . . That's why I'm voting for Obama, no matter what *COPS* has led me to believe about minorities."[21] If you are a white person with little or no personal contact with people of color, and the only depictions of Black people are what you see on TV shows like *COPS*, it's no wonder your perceptions about Black people and culture are disproportionately negative or disapproving.

The issue of representation is also another concern when it comes to the articulation and perpetuation of the white racial frame through popular culture and media. That most shows and films have long centered on white leading characters with almost exclusively white casts reinforces the mistaken notion that whiteness is both normative and ubiquitous. It also presents non-white persons, experiences, and cultures as marginal or exceptional rather than perfectly normal and commonplace. Over the last several years, activists have used social-media campaigns to increase awareness about the underrepresentation and misrepresentation of communities of color in Hollywood.

---

21. Bryan N. Massingale, *Racial Justice and the Catholic Church* (Maryknoll, NY: Orbis Books, 2010), 29.

Such was the aim of the #OscarsSoWhite campaign that journalist April Reign began in 2015.[22] The campaign arose organically in reaction to the nearly exclusively white nominees for all the top awards at the Academy Awards. And this is a prime example of why we must reckon with the fact that racism is, and always has been, a white problem. Who makes television and movies? Who approves the budgets and the scripts, green-lights projects, selects the director, determines the cast, anticipates the market, and so on? The answer is a disproportionately white group of people, and particularly white men.

The systemic racism of the entertainment industry is more consequential than a lot of white people would care to acknowledge. It is, in effect, a functioning "trickle-down economy" of white racial framing that controls what people see and how perceptions are formed. While major entertainment executives are not literally applying "blackface" to represent harmful stereotypes and caricatures of people of color to audiences, as was done in the 1800s, whites are incontrovertibly still the gatekeepers of Black representation to national and global audiences. As long as this is the case, anti-Black racism in popular culture and media remains a white problem, and the supremacy of the white racial frame persists.

Socialization and Implicit Bias

Much of what has been discussed in this chapter can be classified under the general heading of "socialization," which refers to the conscious and unconscious ways we are formed to understand

---

22. Aggi Ashagre, "A Conversation with the Creator of #OscarsSoWhite," *NPR*, January 25, 2016, https://www.npr.org/2016/01/25/464244160/a-conversation-with-the-creator-of-oscarssowhite.

ourselves, others, and the worlds we inhabit. Because this book is focused primarily on the American context (though much of what is contained here applies to other contexts as well), we can say that there are numerous factors that coalesce to shape our socialization. Among these are our immediate and local environments, family rearing, social class, formal and informal education, cultural inputs such as entertainment and media, and others. Just because a grandparent or schoolteacher didn't sit you down and tell you as a white person to think a certain way about another group of people doesn't mean that your upbringing and lifelong education haven't formed your outlook in racialized ways. If you have been born or raised or have lived in the United States for a period of time, then subtle messages and other symbolic signaling have informed your assumptions and biases about others. Most of the examples we have talked about so far have been instances of explicit bias, or at least the explicit manifestation of unconscious socialization. However, it is important for us to name another reason that systemic racism and white privilege are so pervasive and difficult to address head-on at times. That is because there also exists a consequence of our socialization known as "implicit bias," which is extremely subtle and, by definition, difficult to identify directly.

According to a 2015 report by the Kirwan Institute for the Study of Race and Ethnicity at Ohio State University, "Implicit bias refers to the attitudes or stereotypes that affect our understanding, actions, and decisions in an unconscious manner. These biases, which encompass both favorable and unfavorable assessments, are activated involuntarily and without an individual's awareness or intentional control."[23] Implicit bias

---

[23]. Cheryl Staats et al., *State of the Science: Implicit Bias Review 2015* (Columbus, OH: Kirwan Institute, 2015), 62.

is universal; it is found in all people regardless of one's racial, gender, or any other kind of identity. As the report explains, "Everyone is susceptible to implicit biases."[24] The researchers note that the presence of negative implicit bias operates on preconscious levels, which inform our responses to people and circumstances long before conscious thought or discernment is possible. Where the mortal consequences of implicit bias have gained the most public attention in recent years is in policing and the use of deadly force, particularly against unarmed Black women and men. Like all forms of socialization, implicit bias is learned, though it's learned in a far more subtle and unconscious manner. "The implicit associations we harbor in our subconscious cause us to have feelings and attitudes about other people based on characteristics such as race, ethnicity, age, and appearance. These associations are generally believed to develop over the course of a lifetime beginning at a very early age through exposure to direct and indirect messages."[25]

In an effort to help identify what and how these biases operate, researchers describe several key characteristics.[26] For example, implicit biases are "pervasive and robust," meaning that everyone is subject to them and therefore nobody, regardless of stated intention or disposition, is immune from their effect. Implicit biases are related to but nevertheless distinct from those explicit manifestations of bias, prejudice, or stereotyping more readily present to our conscious thought. Implicit biases "do not necessarily align with our declared beliefs," meaning that even white people striving to be better anti-racist allies

---

[24]. Staats et al., *State of the Science*, 62.
[25]. Staats et al., *State of the Science*, 62.
[26]. The following characteristics come from Staats et al., *State of the Science*, 63.

nevertheless are affected by the unconscious associations that have been formed over the course of a lifetime of living in a racist society such as the United States. It is generally the case that implicit biases "favor our own ingroup," though the power of a systemically racist society means that even people of color often can experience some form of internalized racism. Researchers note that implicit biases have "real-world effects on behavior" and that this can range from a physiological fear response when a white person encounters a Black person on the street or in an elevator to far more disturbing and consequential responses such as police officers shooting unarmed people of color for no apparent reason.

Some people find the reality of implicit bias challenging to accept because it seems inherently self-defeating. The reasoning here is that if I am not conscious of these prejudices and assumptions about others, then how can I be expected to change them and how can I be held responsible for them? On the first objection, about our ability to change implicit biases, the good news is that scholars explain that these biases are *malleable*, meaning that just as we have been "wired" at a fundamental and unconscious level to make these kinds of negative associations, we can, in fact, "re-wire" ourselves through unlearning and replacing the racist associations. It is a lot of work, and it is not easy. It requires commitment and effort and deliberation. But it is part of what is necessary to work toward greater racial justice in society, and it is the *agapic* love—that self-sacrificial, other-focused love—that Christ preached, modeled, and demanded of his followers in the gospels.

On this second objection about responsibility, I am reminded of what Rabbi Abraham Joshua Heschel famously wrote in his classic book *The Prophets*. In describing the role of prophets in the community, he explained:

Above all, the prophets remind us of the moral state of a people: *Few are guilty, but all are responsible.* If we admit that the individual is in some measure conditioned or affected by the spirit of society, an individual's crime discloses society's corruption. In a community not indifferent to suffering, uncompromisingly impatient with cruelty and falsehood, continually concerned for God and every man, crime would be infrequent rather than common.[27]

We are all indeed "conditioned or affected by the spirit of society," and as a result it is our *responsibility* to do something about the negative ways we have been so conditioned or affected.

While all people experience implicit bias, my interest here is drawing attention to the ways that systemic racism has conditioned and affected white people far more deeply and more insidiously than typically meets our consciousness. So pervasive is the socialization that it affects us before we realize it and in ways we might not be able to anticipate, particularly if we find ourselves in high-stress situations or unfamiliar circumstances. There are many organizations that offer implicit-bias training to help communities identify and unlearn racist associations acquired over a lifetime of socialization in a systemically racist society. The kind of workshops and programming offered by anti-racist scholars and activists are incredibly useful in helping to name and address the deeply embedded biases that are always already operative beneath our conscious reflection. Parishes are uniquely situated to offer educational and workshop opportunities on systemic racism and implicit bias, and such

---

[27]. Abraham Joshua Heschel, *The Prophets* (New York: HarperCollins, 2001), 19, emphasis added.

offerings could complement longer-term work that is needed among communities that are predominantly white.

Because racism is a white problem, there is also a white responsibility to educate oneself and other white people about it. The only way to counteract a lifetime of racist socialization is to begin learning how to identify such explicit and implicit biases and then begin the hard work of learning to see the world, others, and oneself anew in striving to build a society and Church that prioritize racial justice.

Further Reading

- James Baldwin, *The Cross of Redemption: Uncollected Writings*, ed. Randall Kenan (New York: Vintage Books, 2011).
- James Baldwin, *James Baldwin: Collected Essays*, ed. Toni Morrison (New York: Library of America, 1998).
- Eduardo Bonilla-Silva, *Racism without Racists: Color-Blind Racism and the Persistence of Racial Inequality in America*, 5th ed. (Lanham, MD: Rowman & Littlefield, 2018).
- Laurie M. Cassidy and Alex Mikulich, eds., *Interrupting White Privilege: Catholic Theologians Break the Silence* (Maryknoll, NY: Orbis Books, 2007).
- Michael Eric Dyson, *Tears We Cannot Stop: A Sermon to White America* (New York: St. Martin's Press, 2017).
- Joe R. Feagin, *The White Racial Frame: Centuries of Racial Framing and Counter-Framing*, 3rd ed. (New York: Routledge, 2020).
- Frances E. Kendall, *Understanding White Privilege: Creating Pathways to Authentic Relationships across Race*, 2nd ed. (London: Routledge, 2013).

- Ibram Kendi, *How to Be an Antiracist* (New York: One World, 2019).
- Bryan N. Massingale, "The Assumptions of White Privilege and What We Can Do about It," *National Catholic Reporter*, June 1, 2020.
- Thomas Merton, "Letters to a White Liberal," in *Seeds of Destruction* (New York: Farrar, Straus and Giroux, 1964), 3–71.
- Paula S. Rothenberg, ed., *White Privilege: Essential Readings on the Other Side of Racism*, 5th ed. (New York: Macmillan, 2016).
- Richard Rothstein, *The Color of Law: A Forgotten History of How Our Government Segregated America* (New York: W. W. Norton, 2017).
- Shannon Sullivan, *White Privilege* (Cambridge, UK: Polity Press, 2019).

4

Systems, Structures, and Institutions

One of the greatest deceptions that American society has perpetuated over the decades, through both informal lore and formal historical narrative, is the power of self-sufficiency. Widely held beliefs about meritocracy and stories about people "pulling themselves up by their own bootstraps" have contributed to a sense of self-righteous individualism that has shaped the outlook of a whole nation. White Americans are particularly susceptible to this way of thinking because it contributes to a sense that what one has, what one does, or how one is perceived is accomplished simply on account of one's own efforts and self-determination. Therefore, everything white people experience as a success or accomplishment is attributable to their own agency, and therefore the struggles, suffering, or apparent failures of others are likewise their own fault. Thus, if you are wealthy or powerful or otherwise comfortable, then you deserve it. Conversely, if you are poor or powerless or otherwise disadvantaged, you also deserve it.

However, the old saying about child-rearing—that it "takes a village"—also applies to every other aspect of a person's life in particular and society in general. The seventeenth-century poet John Donne famously summarized this truth in his now-classic

"Meditation 17," penning the often-quoted line: "No man is an island entire of itself; every man is a piece of a continent, a part of the main."[1] Absolutely no one is truly self-sufficient or self-made. Nobody can exist on their own without assistance from another, even if that other is nonhuman. We depend on one another and other creatures for our shelter, clothing, and food. We rely on the companionship of others for emotional and moral support and challenge. We need others in order to live and move and have our being.

On the cosmic scale, I often like to remind folks that none of us photosynthesized our breakfast. We are so inept in a creaturely sense that we cannot do something as basic as take the carbon dioxide of the air, the energy from the sun, and the resources of the soil to produce fuel like plants can. We need to eat plants or eat other creatures that eat plants in order to simply live. On the human scale, we spend the first days, months, and years of our existence 100 percent dependent on other humans to feed, protect, nurture, and teach us how to do the most basic things. A newborn doe is more skilled at merely living than any newborn human; awkward as the doe's first motions are, at least that baby deer can walk!

On the social scale, there are systems, structures, and institutions that predate each of us and make our modern existence possible. That human beings have formed a social contract in which we specialize in different fields, work together and rely on one another's expertise and skills so that we do not have to master everything, and establish rules of social order to facilitate interaction as smoothly as possible is both historically

---

[1.] John Donne, "Meditation 17: Now, This Bell Tolling Softly for Another, Says to Me: Thou Must Die," in *Devotions upon Emergent Occasions and Death's Duel* (New York: Vintage Classics, 1999), 103.

impressive and absolutely necessary. I would not have the time or ability or resources to write this book if other people didn't already design, create, and sell this laptop computer; plant, farm, harvest, package, transport, buy, and prepare the food I had for lunch today; establish and maintain the shared infrastructure (roads, electricity, garbage collection, water treatment and distribution, etc.) upon which I rely for nearly everything but about which I rarely give much thought; and make possible so many other big and little things through our inextricable interdependence.

When you start to lay out all the ways that society functions through systems, structures, and institutions, it quickly becomes obvious how dependent we are on one another. But that basic truth is something that many people—especially white people—are disinclined to acknowledge. Honest reference to the manifold ways in which we are enabled and supported by other people and structures beyond us can threaten the fragile sense that I am solely responsible for my perceived achievements and, by extension, that others are solely responsible for their perceived failures.

In the summer of 2012, President Barack Obama, the first and so far only Black president of the United States, gave a speech in Virginia in which he acknowledged this inescapable and simple fact of our interdependence and reliance on systems, structures, and institutions not of our making.

> There are a lot of wealthy, successful Americans who agree with me—because they want to give something back. They know they didn't—look, if you've been successful, you didn't get there on your own. You didn't get there on your own. I'm always struck by people who think, well, it must be because I was just so smart. There

are a lot of smart people out there. It must be because I worked harder than everybody else. Let me tell you something—there are a whole bunch of hardworking people out there. (Applause.)

If you were successful, somebody along the line gave you some help. There was a great teacher somewhere in your life. Somebody helped to create this unbelievable American system that we have that allowed you to thrive. Somebody invested in roads and bridges. If you've got a business, you didn't build that. Somebody else made that happen. The Internet didn't get invented on its own. Government research created the Internet so that all the companies could make money off the Internet.

The point is, is that when we succeed, we succeed because of our individual initiative, but also because we do things together. There are some things, just like fighting fires, we don't do on our own. I mean, imagine if everybody had their own fire service. That would be a hard way to organize fighting fires.[2]

Not surprisingly, many of President Obama's political rivals used the opportunity of his direct and honest description of our shared interdependence and reliance on government-funded structures and institutions as an occasion to claim that he was attacking the individual success of American citizens. This simple truth is very threatening to those who wish to claim both their own personal achievement and the justified failures or hardships of others.

[2]. Barack Obama, "Remarks by the President at a Campaign Event in Roanoke, Virginia," Office of the White House Press Secretary, July 13, 2012, https://obamawhitehouse.archives.gov/the-press-office/2012/07/13/remarks-president-campaign-event-roanoke-virginia.

But, as Donne wrote, no person is an island floating alone, existing by themselves. We live in a human community, a society made up of webs of relationships that enable and harm, embolden and tear down, support success and facilitate failure—and that community and web of relationships is not neutral. The society in which we find ourselves is, as politicians on both sides of the aisle have come to say frequently, truly *rigged*. Just as men generally benefit and women generally suffer from patriarchal and misogynistic systems, structures, and institutions, so too are whites advantaged and people of color disadvantaged by racist systems, structures, and institutions like those found in the United States. This chapter is a brief exploration of precisely this reality as it plays out in our society and in our Church.

What America Is and Is Not

Less than a month before he would be assassinated at the age of thirty-nine, Martin Luther King Jr. gave a speech in New York to a group of union members, most of whom were people of color. The speech was titled "The Other America," which was the theme of his address. He explained what that subject was all about:

> And I use this subject because there are literally two Americas. One America is flowing with the milk of prosperity and the honey of equality. That America is the habitat of millions of people who have food and material necessities for their bodies, culture and education for their minds, freedom and human dignity for their spirits. That America is made up of millions of young people who grow up in the sunlight of opportunity.[3]

---

3. Martin Luther King Jr., "The Other America," in *The Radical King*, ed. Cornel West (Boston: Beacon Press, 2015), 236.

King goes on to contrast this "first America" with the "other America" of his speech's title:

> But as we assemble here tonight, I'm sure that each of us is painfully aware of the fact that there is another America, and that other America has a daily ugliness about it that transforms the buoyancy of hope into the fatigue of despair. In that other America, millions of people find themselves forced to live in inadequate, substandard, and often dilapidated housing conditions. In these conditions they don't have wall-to-wall carpets, but all too often they find themselves with wall-to-wall rats and roaches. In that other America, thousands, yea, even millions, of young people are forced to attend inadequate, substandard, inferior, quality-less schools, and year after year thousands of young people in this other America finish our high schools reading at an eighth- and a ninth-grade level sometimes. Not because they are dumb, not because they don't have innate intelligence, but because the schools are so inadequate, so overcrowded, so devoid of quality, so segregated, if you will, that the best in these minds can never come out.[4]

What King is describing here is the reality of American society that those who find themselves in the "first America" have been shielded from recognizing, while those condemned to exist in the "second America" have no choice but to confront.

At this point in his public advocacy, King was actively reaching out to poor whites in order to help them see that they too suffered the injustices of systems, structures, and institutions that likewise systemically disadvantaged people of color. One way

---

4. King, "The Other America," 236–37.

a lot of white people attempt to sidestep difficult truths about the injustice of racism and its pervasive presence in American society is to shift one's focus and rhetoric to class issues. It can be a form of denying or ignoring the plight of Black women and men, in particular, by arguing that the *greatest* social ill is not racism but poverty. Martin Luther King Jr. saw the bigger picture and invited whites and Blacks alike to see how social injustice is not easily reducible to financial disparity, though it is part of the puzzle. Historians have noted that King's nonviolent civil rights-era protesting, while discomfiting for many whites in power, was not nearly as threatening to them as his speaking out about the intersecting injustices that also implicate poor whites. While structural injustices have condemned people of color in the United States to this "second America" in an overwhelmingly disproportionate manner—dating back to the enslavement of Africans forced into inescapable servitude and labor—there are actually many white people who find themselves likewise poor and at the margins of society. King was making an effort to awaken and enlist allies from among the poor white communities who also were victims of unjust systems, structures, and institutions that maintained the status quo in order to keep comfortable and well fed those who were located in the "first America."

What was so threatening about this unveiling of the truth King oversaw was how it chipped away at the American myths that white people have told themselves for centuries, typically at the expense of people of color. The primary myth was that of a meritocracy, which claimed that those in the "first America" rightfully belonged there on account of their personal and individual success and moral rectitude, while those in the "second America" likewise deserved their suffering and hardship on account of their laziness or ineptitude. The myth was built on a vision of a nation founded on the principle of white supremacy, which promoted the lie that poor whites always had the chance, if only they worked hard enough and were disciplined enough, to "pull themselves up by their own bootstraps" and enter the "first America" marked, as King put it, by "the milk of prosperity and the honey of equality." But while some poor and marginalized whites existed in the "second America," admittedly in a much lower percentage of the population, the lies of our white supremacist national heritage and the pervasiveness of racist mythology told them that they had a chance, that they weren't like the Black women and men in comparably dire financial straits, and that they were superior to even the best, wealthiest, most successful person of color because they were, despite their precarious state, *white*.

In that insightful 1968 speech, King makes a number of powerful observations, many of which sadly still ring as true today as they did a half century ago. One example is the way America creates popular myths that distinguish whites and Blacks in similar economic circumstances: "When there is massive unemployment in the black community, it's called a social problem. But when there is massive unemployment in the white community, it's called a depression. With the black man, it's 'welfare,' with the whites, it's 'subsidies.' This country has socialism for the rich, rugged individualism for the poor."[5] One of the reasons that systemic racism and white privilege persist in this country—despite the fact that many times economic and class injustice reaches across the color line—is that our culture maintains a false sense of white supremacy: a sense of superiority that not only feeds an unrealistic aspiration on the part of poor whites that they can one day ascend to the "first America," but

---

5. King, "The Other America," 237.

even while they remain in the "second America" they can be thankful that at least they are not Black.

What is instructive about King's powerful legacy and rhetoric, which is all too often softened or whitewashed for white comfort, is that he continually challenges white Americans to question the myths and historical narratives they tell themselves about themselves and others. American exceptionalism, American meritocracy, American white supremacy—these are all lies, each of which also harms whites while these lies overtly subjugate and oppress people of color. But for any white person who finds oneself in a precarious social location, a sense of false superiority and the grasping on to a false hope for social ascendency at the expense of people of color is appealing. It is for this reason that politicians, particularly those who have affiliated with the far right, have used race as a touchstone of policies that support the wealthy, who are overwhelmingly white, and disadvantage the poor, who are overwhelmingly people of color.

In an infamous interview with political-science scholar Alexander Lamis, Lee Atwater, one of President Ronald Reagan's campaign consultants, explained in graphic detail the simple logic behind some of the political right's social policies that expressly disadvantage people of color. Even though many of these same policies ultimately harm poor whites in the process, the racist undercurrent signaled in the policy formation taps into the unexamined American myths that whites tell themselves. Repeatedly using an anti-Black racial slur, Atwater famously explained:

> You start out in 1954 by saying, "N****r, n****r, n****r." By 1968 you can't say "n****r"—that hurts you, backfires. So you say stuff like, uh, forced busing, states' rights, and all that stuff, and you're getting so abstract.

Now, you're talking about cutting taxes, and all these things you're talking about are totally economic things and a byproduct of them is, blacks get hurt worse than whites.... "We want to cut this," is much more abstract than even the busing thing, uh, and a hell of a lot more abstract than "N****r, n****r."[6]

This sort of political machination, which persists in more recent racist slogans like "Make America Great Again," attempts to shore up the benefits accrued by those in what King called the "first America" while playing poor whites against people of color. The "MAGA" slogan also suggests that in times past things were preferable, better, or ideal, not so subtly suggesting that the advancements that people of color have achieved in our historically racist society ought to be erased. It elicits a false nostalgia about erstwhile better times that for white, straight, cisgender men may have been okay, but for anybody else were certainly less great than today (and we still have a long way to go in terms of justice and equality for all).

When I was growing up, as a white kid in a largely white community, I was taught in my private Catholic schools that America was founded as a "melting pot," a metaphor invoked to suggest the benefits of immigrant assimilation and the formation of a nation that brought together folks of diverse heritages and cultures into one new nation. But the fact of the matter is that this has never been an accurate depiction, at any point in history, of the American context. Yes, assimilation was always promoted,

---

6. Quoted in Rick Perlstein, "Lee Atwater's Infamous 1981 Interview on the Southern Strategy," *The Nation*, November 13, 2012, https://www.thenation.com/article/archive/exclusive-lee-atwaters-infamous-1981-interview-southern-strategy. [Author note: I have censored the use of the n-word in this quote.]

tacitly and directly, and it was what motivated certain groups of white European descent to adopt a new language and customs in an effort to "belong." But there have always been minoritized populations, those for whom the myth of progress from the "second America" to the "first America" was always a foreclosed possibility. In subsequent years, in an effort to shift from the glorification of assimilation to respect for a more multicultural society, I have heard teachers and politicians refer to America as a "stew" rather than a "melting pot." Such a stew, the narrative goes, includes everybody in the same pot but does not *melt* the distinctive features and character of each ingredient, instead allowing them to exist side by side and, in theory, enhance the flavor of the other collected ingredients. I suppose this stovetop analogy is an improvement on the melting-pot hegemony, but it still doesn't account for those "ingredients" that are precluded from entering the community pot from the outset. This is where Martin Luther King Jr.'s point about "two Americas" is so important, for it holds up a critical mirror to all in society and invites a difficult but necessary reflection on our context as it actually is rather than as we would like to believe it to be.

The key point here is that inequality, racism, and white privilege are neither coincidental nor unintentional. There are systems, policies, laws, enforcement, structures, institutions, and customs that establish and reinforce the disparity between the (at least) *two* Americas that exist in reality. Part of what it means to be engaged in working for justice and peace, particularly as a Catholic Christian, is to avoid shying away from painful truths such as these. It means coming to terms with the fact that the way you experience the world, understand history, and narrate your American experience, especially if you are white, is not necessarily the way others do. Rather than form new ways to metaphorically describe the pot in which you happen to find yourself, it is better to look outside the pot to see who is excluded from the beginning and how people in that context experience the world as very different from your own.

Racial Profiling and Police Brutality

In the summer of 2013 a federal judge from the United States District Court for the Southern District of New York ruled that New York City's controversial "stop and frisk" policy was unconstitutional.[7] At first glance, the content of the New York City police department's policy seems reasonable and not immediately tied to issues of race or racism. According to the *Washington Post*, the policy stated that "police will detain and question pedestrians, and potentially search them, if they have a 'reasonable suspicion' that the pedestrian in question 'committed, is committing, or is about to commit a felony or a Penal Law misdemeanor.'"[8] Again, the language appears race and gender neutral. But as we saw earlier in this chapter with the disturbingly frank quote from Lee Atwater describing Republican political agendas that intentionally target Blacks and other people of color under the euphemistic guise of "law and order," the "stop and frisk" policy in New York likewise appeared one way on paper and another in practice.

[7.] Aaron Blake, "Judge Says New York's 'Stop and Frisk' Law Unconstitutional," *Washington Post*, August 12, 2013, https://www.washingtonpost. com/news/post-politics/wp/2013/08/12/judge-says-new-yorks-stop-and-frisk-law-unconstitutional/?arc404=true.

[8.] Dylan Matthews, "Here's What You Need to Know about Stop and Frisk—and Why the Courts Shut It Down," *Washington Post*, August 13, 2013, https://www.washingtonpost.com/news/wonk/wp/2013/08/13/heres-what-you-need-to-know-about-stop-and-frisk-and-why-the-courts-shut-it-down/.

What one does not see in the wording of the policy is the manner in which it was executed to disproportionately target Black and Hispanic people in New York City. Looking at the data from one year prior to the court's ruling of the policy's unconstitutionality, in 2012 the combined Black and Hispanic population was approximately 54 percent of that of New York City as a whole. However, this population constituted 84 percent of those subjected to the "stop and frisk" policy—in other words, those detained by police without a warrant. Meanwhile, the white population made up approximately 33 percent of the city's total population, but whites only made up about 10 percent of those detained on the grounds of "stop and frisk."[9] Then-Mayor Michael Bloomberg defended the policy (which he later reluctantly walked back from during his short-lived 2020 presidential campaign) by claiming that focusing on areas high in crime explains the racial disparities. However, scholars—such as Jeffrey Fagan of Columbia University—point out that even if you control for the crime rate, "the racial makeup of a precinct is a good predictor of the number of stops."[10] Additionally, studies submitted to the court reveal that the return on investment in the policy was negligible in terms of actual arrests and citations. Despite the mayor's ardent defense of the policy and its supposed causation

---

[9]. Matthews, "Here's What You Need to Know about Stop and Frisk." See also Jaeah Lee and Adam Serwer, "Charts: Are the NYPD's Stop-and-Frisks Violating the Constitution?," *Mother Jones*, April 29, 2013, https://www.motherjones.com/politics/2013/04/new-york-nypd-stop-frisk-lawsuit-trial-charts/.

[10]. Matthews, "Here's What You Need to Know about Stop and Frisk." See also "Report of Jeffrey Fagan, Ph.D.," submitted in the case *David Floyd et al. v. City of New York et al.*, 08 Civ. 1034 (SAS) (S.D. N.Y. October 2008).

in declining crime rates (which is a phenomenon reflected in nationwide trends, including jurisdictions that never engaged in such unconstitutional practices), the policy appears simply to have served as a justification for New York law enforcement to unjustly target communities of color. While decreasing crime rates can be attributable to other factors, one indisputable consequence of the policy in New York was the further alienation of communities of color as they were singly targeted for this kind of systemic and institutional harassment.[11]

We have already seen in earlier chapters of this book how laws and policies, often drafted and implemented by white people in power, are frequently framed in a manner that on the surface appears "reasonable" or "logical." The narrative that many such well-meaning individuals tell themselves is that what they are inaugurating is a "color-blind" law that seeks merely to protect the common good and maintain social order. But in practice, many of these kinds of laws and policies disproportionately affect people of color, leading to an increase of harassment by law enforcement at best and brutality or murder at worst. Police officers are no different from the rest of the population in the sense that they too have been socialized in a racist and white supremacist culture.[12] Racial profiling can be an overt policy, something that harkens back to the Jim Crow era of "law

---

[11]. For a scientific analysis of the unintended deleterious and long-term consequences of "stop and frisk" policies on communities of color, see David Weisburd, Cody W. Telep, and Brian A. Lawton, "Could Innovations in Policing Have Contributed to the New York City Crime Drop Even in a Period of Declining Police Strength? The Case of Stop, Question, and Frisk as a Hot Spots Policing Strategy," *Justice Quarterly* 31 (2014): 129–53.

[12]. See Lynne Peeples, "Brutality and Racial Bias: What the Data Say," *Nature* 583 (July 2, 2020): 22–24.

enforcement" in the southern United States or in the redlining housing policies of the northern states.

But racial profiling is also manifested in far more covert and even tacit ways. Recall the previous section on "implicit bias," wherein some prejudices and racialized assumptions operate in a preconscious manner. If you are a white person like me, who has grown up in a society such as is found throughout the United States, have you found yourself in a situation where you notice biological triggers—increased heart rate, adrenaline rush, even sweating—when you unexpectedly encounter a person of color? If so, then you already know on some level the complex phenomena that affect a white police officer or other persons in authority when they are confronting a person of color. That is an illustration of implicit bias and the preconscious yet learned response to certain populations of people that can result in violence and even death. Additionally, given the pervasiveness of racist socialization in the American context, it is important also to note that people of color are oftentimes themselves victims of internalized racism. Just because an officer of color perpetuates intimidation or harassment or violence against a civilian of color does not, in any way, mean that racism isn't involved. Racism, as we discussed in the first chapter, is about *power*, not just one's phenotype or perceived skin color.[13]

Not everyone is as expressly racist as Lee Atwater and the politicians he advised. Most white people don't actually think about these kinds of laws and policies very much at all, unless they happen upon a news story or are otherwise forced to

---

13. For an illustration of racialized sexual violence as an exercise of power at the hands of law enforcement, see Bryan N. Massingale, "The Erotic Life of Anti-Blackness: Police Sexual Violation of Black Bodies," in *Anti-Blackness and Christian Ethics*, ed. Vincent W. Lloyd and Andrew Prevot (Maryknoll, NY: Orbis Books, 2017), 173–94.

think about such issues. This is yet another unearned benefit of white privilege—the freedom from concern about the unequal application of the law and the deliberate targeting of innocent civilians. Many white people unconsciously exercise their privilege and willful ignorance about the racist nature of our social systems, structures, and institutions when they assess a complex situation like New York's "stop and frisk" policy from the "letter of the law" alone. White people frequently take comfort in the words on the page without much consideration for the disparity of its application. This is likewise the case when many whites hear about arrests for drug possession or nonviolent crimes for which whites are rarely arrested or convicted, but which whites are statistically just as likely to perpetrate. White privilege is the condition of the very possibility that one could live in New York City and be generally oblivious to the racist plight that faces people of color on a daily basis, constantly threatening them with at least harassment or inconvenience and even threatening their lives.

This latter point about the persistence of the threat to one's life and safety has been on wider display in recent years in terms of police brutality. For many, if not most, American whites, instances of police brutality against people of color have been understood as a rare but unfortunate consequence of law enforcement. The widely viewed video recording of the Los Angeles police beating Rodney King, an unarmed Black man, in March 1991 was one of the first contemporary instances, in a pre-internet era, of the whole nation and world being confronted with the reality of police brutality. The truth is, that last sentence needs further qualification—it was one of the first instances in which the *white population* of America and others around the globe were forced to reckon with a reality that people of color have known in this nation since before its founding.

Legal scholar Michelle Alexander, in her important and influential 2010 book, *The New Jim Crow: Mass Incarceration in the Age of Colorblindness*, opens her study of the emergence of the contemporary racialized mass incarceration system in the United States with a historical survey of the American legal system's treatment of Black women and men.[14] Alexander makes the bold yet historically grounded case that in addition to the so-called class system we have in the United States ("working," "middle," "upper," etc.), we also have a distinctive racial *caste* system, according to which certain populations are permanently barred from full equality, flourishing, and advancement in society. More recently, the Pulitzer Prize–winning author Isabel Wilkerson has compellingly argued that this framework of "caste" best describes the racist structure of our American society.[15] Black women and men in what is now the United States have been systematically subjugated and placed en masse into an "undercaste" from 1619, when the first enslaved Africans were brought to North American shores, onward. Over the last four centuries, despite what many whites have been led to believe or have convinced themselves to be true, women and men of African descent have not *coincidentally* had a tough time surviving and succeeding in American society; no, it has been a very *deliberate and conscious* series of systems, structures, and institutions that have—in succession—kept Blacks in this American "undercaste" at each period of American history. As Alexander recounts, first it was the birth of chattel slavery, then it was the birth of the Jim Crow era, and then it was the birth of the era of mass incarceration. These are not discrete phenomena

---

[14]. Michelle Alexander, *The New Jim Crow: Mass Incarceration in the Age of Colorblindness* (New York: New Press, 2010).

[15]. See Isabel Wilkerson, *Caste: The Origins of Our Discontents* (New York: Random House, 2020).

that merely chanced to take place or emerged organically as if by the laws of nature. They are epochal periods of American history that correspond to deliberate racist systems such as chattel slavery, racist structures such as the written and unwritten laws and norms of the Jim Crow era, and racist institutions such as the ironically named "criminal *justice* system" of the United States. Distinctive though each might be in particular detail and historical moment, all of them reflect an uncomfortable truth and painful reality about American society: racism is woven deep within who it is we actually are as a community and how it is we actually exist as a society.

Alexander summarizes this foundational insight well:

> White supremacy, over time, became a religion of sorts. Faith in the idea that people of the African race were bestial, that whites were inherently superior, and that slavery was, in fact, for blacks' own good, served to alleviate the white conscience and reconcile the tension between slavery and the democratic ideals espoused by whites in the so-called New World.[16]

Sometimes referred to as "America's Original Sin," this racist worldview was embedded in the very same DNA that marks the principles and aspirations of the United States.[17] White supremacy is like a genetic disease that is passed on from one generation to the next, while always being bolstered, protected, and perpetuated by the manner in which American systems, structures, and institutions are run and laws and policies applied.

---

[16]. Alexander, *New Jim Crow*, 26.
[17]. See Jim Wallis, *America's Original Sin: Racism, White Privilege, and the Bridge to a New America* (Grand Rapids, MI: Brazos Press, 2016).

Returning to that horrifying video of the police beating of Rodney King in 1991, and the subsequent acquittal of the police officers who participated in that state-sanctioned act of brutality, the only thing exceptional about that show of racialized violence and force was that it was captured on camera. For the last two decades, in the wake of smartphone technology, most adult Americans are walking around with a computer, camera, and internet source in their pockets or purses. As a result, there has been a steady increase of videos capturing flagrant instances of police brutality, overwhelmingly targeting women, men, and children of color. Again, it's not that this is a new phenomenon; it's just that many white people are now unable to brush off or ignore the stark and plain reality that haunts the daily existence of people of color in the United States. (Perhaps it was your own encounter with one or more of these disturbing videos that led you to pick up this very book to learn more about racism and privilege.)

The historian Khalil Gibran Muhammad demonstrates in his 2010 book, *The Condemnation of Blackness: Race, Crime, and the Making of Modern Urban America*, just how deeply intertwined law enforcement and racism are and have been in the United States.[18] The most important thing for white people to realize is that the proliferation of viral videos capturing police brutality is not merely a series of one-off cases or instances of a few "bad apple" police officers. Police brutality, like the racial profiling that disproportionately targets people of color, is a structural problem. And it is the responsibility of white people, by virtue of our privileged places in this racist society, to recognize the

---

[18]. Khalil Gibran Muhammad, *The Condemnation of Blackness: Race, Crime, and the Making of Modern Urban America* (Cambridge, MA: Harvard University Press, 2010).

systemic oppression, subjugation, and brutalization of Black children, women, and men in this country. This is seen no more clearly than in the American prison system.

Mass Incarceration

The not-so-subtle racist agenda of some American politicians in the second half of the twentieth century, which was illustrated by Atwater's blunt and disturbing admission cited earlier, began in the late 1950s and has continued up through the present. One of the most recognizable slogans of this era is "law and order," which, as Michelle Alexander explains, "was first mobilized in the late 1950s as Southern governors and law enforcement officials attempted to generate and mobilize white opposition to the Civil Rights Movement."[19] With the impending death of the last vestiges of Jim Crow signaled by key US Supreme Court decisions such as *Brown v. Board of Education* (1954) and the passage of legislation like the Civil Rights Act in 1964, the perpetuation of white supremacy and systemic racism required yet another transformation if whites wanted to maintain some semblance of the status quo that oppressed Blacks and other people of color. The solution was the creation in the 1980s of a positive-sounding and seemingly innocuous campaign for social order and safety called the "War on Drugs."

For many white readers, this unveiling of the deeper meaning of the slogan "War on Drugs" might be disturbing, and your inclination may be defensiveness. You may think that there is nothing "inherently racist" about a focused effort to root out the illegal drug trade and related crime, but this is exactly the intention behind what Alexander and other scholars

---

[19]. Alexander, *New Jim Crow*, 40.

have noted was a solution without an immediate problem. The "War on Drugs" was announced *prior* to a rise in so-called inner-city drug problems, such as what would be later associated with the crack cocaine fixation of politicians and media alike. Furthermore, political programs like the "War on Drugs" would indeed be a theoretical good use of resources if it were in fact color-blind, but like many American laws and the institution of American policing itself, it was deployed in an overwhelmingly disproportionate way against Blacks and other people of color. As Alexander summarizes, "The War on Drugs, cloaked in race-neutral language, offered whites opposed to racial reform a unique opportunity to express their hostility towards blacks and black progress, without being exposed to the charge of racism."[20] There was also a whole range of affiliated racist-coded phrases that accompanied the "War on Drugs" and that singled out people of color. Such derogatory terms include "welfare queen," "crack whore," "crack baby," and "super-predators," among others. Notice that none of these offensive phrases overtly identifies its target's race, but like the "War on Drugs" and other euphemisms such as "inner city" or even "the ghetto," the intended object of derision is clear.

It is one thing to announce a "War on Drugs" in theory, and an entirely other thing to see how it is implemented in practice. Showing how such campaigns are deployed as a form of social control and oppression is what Alexander's book *The New Jim Crow* does so painstakingly. For the better part of the last half century, federal and local legislators have taken the occasion to fight the "War on Drugs" as cover to pass draconian laws that, in practice if not always in the legislative text, disproportionately target and harm people of color. During this time, "ninety

---

[20]. Alexander, *New Jim Crow*, 54.

percent of those admitted to prison for drug offenses in many states were black or Latino, yet the mass incarceration of communities of color was explained in race-neutral terms, an adaptation to the needs and demands of the current political climate."[21] The overt racism of the Jim Crow era was no longer socially or politically tolerable, and so the "War on Drugs" with its associated mandatory minimum sentences and "three strikes laws," which forced judges to treat repeat nonviolent drug offenders as if they committed a capital crime after multiple drug charges, created a pipeline of Black and Brown bodies cycling in and out of the American prison system.

What is important to realize here is, again, that this is not a matter of happenstance, as if Black people are *coincidentally* more likely than whites to use, abuse, or sell illegal drugs. In fact, the sociological and criminological data show quite a different picture: whites are as likely as—and in some cases, *more likely* than—Blacks to use, abuse, or sell illegal drugs.[22] So why are there so many Black people, particularly Black men and teenagers, in prison, particularly on ostensible drug charges? The uncomfortable answer is that it is because they are *targeted* and often disadvantaged throughout the process of navigating the justice system because people of color are statistically less likely to have the resources that whites, facing comparable crimes and misdemeanors, typically do to fight charges or negotiate sentences with prosecutors. Furthermore, even those who are able to afford good legal counsel are nonetheless marked by

---

[21]. Alexander, *New Jim Crow*, 58.

[22]. For more, see Doris Marie Provine, *Unequal under Law: Race in the War on Drugs* (Chicago: University of Chicago Press, 2007); Human Rights Watch, "Punishment and Prejudice: Racial Disparities in the War on Drugs," *HRW Reports* 12, no. 2 (May 2000), https://www.hrw.org/reports/2000/usa; and Alexander, *New Jim Crow*, 275n10.

the racist presumption of guilt because of the collective social imaginary that is narrated in the media, in entertainment, and in other mechanisms of socialization. Prosecutors, judges, and juries are not exempt from the effects of that socialization.

But it is not simply the creation of a specious "War on Drugs" that has led to the astronomical rise in American incarceration rates, especially for the disproportionate percentage of that population that is Black; it is the whole criminal justice system through and through. As historian Muhammad puts it, "The idea of black criminality was crucial to the making of modern urban America."[23] The stories told personally or via entertainment media and the stereotypes presumed to be universal that arose from such depictions of Black people as inherently "criminal" reinforced white (and sometimes even Black) support for a system of injustice that is cold, calculating, and designed to maintain a social structure of white supremacy. The consequences of mass incarceration of people of color, this "New Jim Crow," are long-lasting and detrimental to whole communities. Michelle Alexander notes in her study how many white and Black people alike are quick to reinforce stereotypes about Black family units, making sweeping claims about "absentee fathers" or promiscuous "baby mamas" without looking beyond the hyperbolized and racialized rhetoric to see what is behind the kernel of truth contained in the observation that Black men are "missing" from the scene. Where have they gone? Is it simply irresponsibility or laziness? No. The absence of a significant population of Black men is due to an unjust criminal justice system that is designed to subjugate and control this population, while perpetuating the "undercaste" that Alexander described earlier.

---

23. Muhammad, *Condemnation of Blackness*, 272.

As white people, it is our responsibility to educate ourselves by means of the resources and access to power that our unearned privilege affords us in an unjust society. Sadly, most white people are either indifferent, wrongly convinced that mass incarceration doesn't impact them, or willfully in denial. Alexander summarizes: "Today, most Americans know and don't know the truth about mass incarceration. For more than three decades, images of black men in handcuffs have been a regular staple of the evening news."[24] This powerful and repeated depiction of Black criminality bolsters white ignorance and reinforces a mistaken sense that people of color must naturally be deserving of imprisonment. "We tell ourselves they 'deserve' their fate, even though we know—and don't know—that whites are just as likely to commit many crimes, especially drug crimes. We know that people released from prison face a lifetime of discrimination, scorn, and exclusion, and yet we claim not to know that an undercaste exists. We know and we don't know at the same time."[25]

The key is for everybody, but especially white people, to look deeper, ask questions, examine the mechanisms at work, and come to see the painful truth and disturbing reality that the extremely high incarceration rates for Black people and other people of color are not accidental, patently deserved, or coincidental. The criminal justice system in the United States is itself designed to appear orderly and "fair" from the outside, but on the inside it is a system of racialized control and oppression. The prison system is but one stark illustration of this kind of structural and institutional injustice; sadly, so also is the Catholic Church in the United States.

---

[24]. Alexander, *New Jim Crow*, 182.
[25]. Alexander, *New Jim Crow*, 182.

Racism and the Catholic Church

The eminent Catholic theologian M. Shawn Copeland explains that, when it comes to racism and the manner in which whiteness functions in systems, structures, and institutions, "as an ideology, white racist supremacy maintains that white people should direct, rule, govern, and dominate nonwhite peoples in *all* cultural, societal, and religious domains."[26] So far in this chapter, we have looked at the manner in which systems, structures, and institutions are affected by the pervasive, organized, and insidious nature of white supremacy at the broadly civil and social levels. But as Copeland notes, this is true in *"all . . . domains,"* including the Church. That many white Catholics reading this might be shocked to consider the systemic racism of the Catholic Church in America reflects not the novelty of the observation, but the shielding that white Catholics have long received from this truth. The shielding whites have received is a result of white privilege and the benefits of presumed white normativity. If everything you experience in church, from music and artwork to homily topics and social interests, aligns with what you already presuppose to be "traditional" or "true" or "universal," then it's clear that you may not on your own come to see the power and consequence of white supremacy operative in the Church. You already fit in, you already feel comfortable, and you are not subject to challenge or testing.

However, this systemic racism of the Catholic Church in America is something that Black Catholics have known and experienced their entire lives. In 1968 a group of Black Roman Catholic clergy formed an organization called the National Black

---

[26]. M. Shawn Copeland, "White Supremacy and Anti-Black Logics in the Making of U.S. Catholicism," in *Anti-Blackness and Christian Ethics*, 65, emphasis original.

Catholic Clergy Caucus (NBCCC).[27] The organization serves an important role for the Church in America in that it offers both a supportive group for Black ministers in the Church—which is a proportionately small minority of the total number of ordained Catholic deacons, priests, and bishops in the United States—and an advocacy group for issues related to Catholics of African descent, which is a demographic group not often prioritized by the overwhelmingly white Catholic leadership in the United States. The opening line of the founding statement drafted in 1968 names an uncomfortable truth about the Catholic Church in America that most white Catholics would rather not consider: "The Catholic Church in the United States, primarily a white racist institution, has addressed itself primarily to white society and is definitely part of that society."[28]

---

[27]. The National Black Catholic Clergy Caucus mission statement reads: "The primary purpose of the NBCCC is to serve God and when we serve him we allow God to speak and act through us. We serve as the voice of those who are at the bottom of our society. We struggle with our brothers and sister [sic] and our collective hope is the struggle. We take a fundamental stand against the ills of society that produce the ditches that the poorest people inhabit. We stand in solidarity with them and serve as a voice crying out in the wilderness for social justice. We work to transform the minds and consciousness of the weak and powerless and have a special proclivity for our African-American brothers and sisters. We provide fish when we can and point them to where the fish are when we can't. We teach the folks we serve how to fish for themselves. We reach back in our history from Africa through the Diaspora and we celebrate our giftedness and our identity and our spirit of survival. We celebrate our liturgies and our lives and we do whatever is necessary to spread the Good News of Jesus Christ through our Words, our Sacraments and our Lives." For more information, visit the organization's website: http://www.tnbccc.com.

[28]. "A Statement of the Black Catholic Clergy Caucus," in *Black Theology: A Documentary History, 1966–1979*, ed. James H. Cone and Gayraud S. Wilmore, vol. 1 (Maryknoll, NY: Orbis Books, 1993), 230.

This direct and powerful statement from the NBCCC reflects an indisputable if disturbing reality that stems from the Catholic Church's long-standing complicity in perpetuating the lie of white supremacy and maintaining the oppression of BIPOC. While we will explore the Church's formal statements and teachings on race and racism in the next chapter, it is worth pausing here to consider three ways in which the Catholic Church in the United States has operated as a "white racist institution," as the NBCCC rightly describes it.

First, simply as an institution composed of sinful human beings in the world, the Catholic Church in the United States cannot help but be shaped in its systems, structures, and institutions by the very same forces that operate on its members in other spheres of society and culture. This dynamic relationship between the so-called world and the Church was affirmed by the Second Vatican Council (1962–1965), which serves as the Catholic Church's highest authority on the topic. The title of its groundbreaking and influential 1965 document *Gaudium et Spes* makes this plain, for it is named "The Pastoral Constitution on the *Church in the Modern World.*" The truth expressed here is that one cannot conceive of the Catholic Church as some kind of alternative society or hermetically sealed community, but it is always already shaped, influenced, formed, and affected by the very same factors that shape, influence, form, and affect its members—all the baptized, both those in formal ministry and the laity.

That the Catholic Church exists in the context of a particular place, such as the United States of America, means that those factors that compose the social, political, and cultural identity of the context also impact the Church. As Bryan Massingale explains, "Racism, at its core, is a set of meanings and values that informs the American way of life. It is a way of understanding and interpreting skin color differences so that white Americans enjoy a privileged social status with access to advantages and benefits to the detriment, disadvantage, and burden of persons of color."[29] Because this racist "set of meanings and values" informs the social and cultural context of the United States, it also informs the social and cultural context of the Catholic Church here. While this is historically and sociologically understandable, like all instances of racism, it is not inevitable. Rather, at each historical moment over the last four centuries, Catholics—especially Catholic leaders—have made choices in which the Church as a structure and institution has protected and promoted white supremacy and racial injustice, oftentimes under the disturbing and disingenuous guise of "God's will." As Massingale observes, "Rather than rejoicing in the God-given diversity of the human family, too often Catholics reflect the racial attitudes and divisions of U.S. society."[30]

The manner in which this racist culture in the American Church has been manifested varies according to time and place. At times, this included overt participation in and direct benefit from the slave economy of the American South. As Copeland recounts,

> In the upper and lower South, Catholic slaveholders lived alongside their Protestant planter counterparts. Some Catholic families thrived in the South, owning slaves, achieving great wealth, professional success, and sociopolitical status. Religious orders of women and men owned human property: the Carmelites, Jesuits,

---

[29] Bryan N. Massingale, *Racial Justice and the Catholic Church* (Maryknoll, NY: Orbis Books, 2010), 42.

[30] Massingale, *Racial Justice and the Catholic Church*, 45.

and Sulpicians in Maryland; Ursulines, Religious of the Sacred Heart, and Capuchins in Louisiana; the Visitation nuns in Washington, D.C.; Dominicans, Sisters of Charity, and Sisters of Loretto in Kentucky; the Vincentians in Missouri.[31]

Other times, up to and including our own time, the Catholic Church was more tacit in its complicity in white racist supremacy, such as in what it *did not do* and *did not say* as an institution. Such is the case in refusing to admit people of color into full and active participation and life in the Church, as well as precluding people of color from entering religious life and serving in positions of Church leadership. Copeland explains:

> The hierarchy held (and holds) interpretative and juridical power to justify geographic and spatial sequestering or segregation of black flesh and bodies. Their accommodation to anti-black logics included the establishment of segregated parishes, schools, and, in some cases, cemeteries; the denial, exclusion, and prohibition of black bodies from religious vows and from priesthood; and the proscription of black religious expressive culture and spirituality.[32]

While some of these explicit policies of discrimination and segregation are no longer legal in a civil sense nor overtly practiced in the Church, the consequences of systemic, structural, and institutional racism continue to affect the

---

[31]. Copeland, "White Supremacy and Anti-Black Logics in the Making of U.S. Catholicism," 69.

[32]. Copeland, "White Supremacy and Anti-Black Logics in the Making of U.S. Catholicism," 73–74.

policies, practices, and priorities of the Catholic Church in the United States. As Massingale notes, "The enduring residential segregation of U.S. society is mirrored in the racial and ethnic composition of Catholic parishes, which are often geographically based and thus reflect the racial and economic disparities of our nation's neighborhoods."[33]

The second way in which the Catholic Church in the United States continues to operate as a "white racist institution" is in its collective and uncritical appropriation of white normativity. In chapter 2 we examined the ways in which American society and culture is shaped by a presumption of whiteness as the norm, which then has a deleterious impact on people of color while simultaneously bolstering a sense of white privilege for those who conform to those ideals. The same dynamic continues to be at play in the Church. Massingale explains that the Church as a "white racist institution" means "more than the obvious fact that a Western European culture has shaped the culture of the Catholic Church in the United States. What makes this a 'white' church culture is deeper than the cultural roots of its liturgical music and rubrics. It is the presumption that these—and *only* these—particular cultural expressions are standard, normative, universal, and thus really 'Catholic.'"[34]

In a 1997 address to the National Black Catholic Congress, Bishop Edward Braxton, then-bishop of Belleville, Illinois, spoke about the "cultural divide" that exists between the way that the Catholic Church in America has understood and presented itself as a predominantly white institution and the life, experience, and culture of African Americans in general and Black Catholics in particular. While to many white Catholics it might seem

---

[33]. Massingale, *Racial Justice and the Catholic Church*, 45.
[34]. Massingale, *Racial Justice and the Catholic Church*, 79.

trivial or unimportant to focus on art and devotional imagery in our Catholic spaces as an illustration of this cultural divide, it does offer a stark and literally illustrative presentation of the sort of white normativity that pervades American Catholicism in some visible and myriad unseen ways.

In his remarks, Braxton recounted a conversation he had with a Black seminarian who had just left formation for the priesthood out of disillusionment and frustration. One of the things that this young man reflected on in his discussion with the bishop was the hegemony of white Christian art everywhere in the Catholic Church. From angels (which, theologically speaking, are immaterial creatures and therefore *do not have any color skin*) and saints to the Holy Family itself (a Middle Eastern Jewish family that certainly would not have had blond hair and blue eyes), stained glass, icons, paintings, and statues all seem to reinforce whiteness as both normative and the only visible representation of sanctity. Braxton recounted a series of rhetorical questions the young Black man asked, which cut right to the heart of the Church's full embrace of white normativity and the significance of that exclusionary worldview when the situation is hypothetically flipped.

> What if the situation were reversed? How would Catholics of European origin feel if, starting tomorrow, all of the images of the Trinity, Jesus, Mary, saints, angels and all the inhabitants of heaven in their churches had black, Hispanic, Asian or Native American features and none were white? Would they feel fully at home and welcome? Is this not what black Catholics have lived with for generations? Is this not what they are going to live with for generations to come? Surely, the total absence of images of the holy and the sacred from a black

perspective in our churches has a negative impact on the church's efforts to evangelize black Americans. The image of a magnificent black angel in a cathedral might do more for the evangelization of black people than handing out copies of a prayer book at the door. Who would want to join a faith in which all the spiritual "personalities" are visualized to look like the very people who enslaved and oppressed them?[35]

Obviously, the ubiquity of white Christian art is not the only or even the most egregious iteration of the Catholic Church's uncritical embrace and proliferation of whiteness as normative. But it does shine a light on something immediately recognizable, thereby typifying the more insidious reality of white supremacy and racism in the Church. As Massingale summarizes, these kinds of overt examples of white exclusivity "illustrate the fundamental insight that in a white racist church, 'Catholic' means 'white.' In U.S. Catholicism, only European aesthetics and cultural products are truly Catholic—regardless of the church's rhetorical commitment to universality."[36]

The consequences of the Catholic Church's white exclusivity are not limited only to artistic and liturgical aesthetics but also reach to the stories we tell ourselves about the saints we admire and to whom we pray. The work of Catholic ethicist Katie Walker Grimes on the historical narratives passed down about canonized saints who are remembered for their apparent valiant defense of and support for people of color is instructive here. Grimes's research unveils how the Church's telling of the lives of

---

[35]. Edward Braxton, "Evangelization: Crossing the Cultural Divide," *Origins* 27 (October 2, 1997): 277.

[36]. Massingale, *Racial Justice and the Catholic Church*, 81.

Peter Claver and Martín de Porres offers historically distorted perspectives. The popular depiction of both men portrays them as seventeenth-century heroes "to black slaves and their racialized descendants" in the newly colonized Americas.[37] Grimes explains the uncomfortable truth about both saints, which has been covered over by pious hagiographies and rewritten to protect white comfort.

> But in truth neither man deemed Africanized slavery to be evil; nor apparently has the church: it has not considered opposition to black slavery either a sign of holiness or a requirement for it. Even worse, both Claver and Porres appeared extraordinarily holy to their earliest advocates not because they challenged and destabilized the regnant racial order but precisely for the ways they held it together. Rather than protecting black slaves from slavery as his champions claim, Claver instead helped to incorporate them into it. And rather than using Christian humility in order to subvert the racial order, Porres enacted a racially bifurcated version of it. Both sainthoods also helped to fashion and justify a distinctly Catholic theology of Africanized slavery in which re-fashioned supposedly racially neutral Catholic virtues such as humility, love, respect for authority, and peace accorded with the logic of racialized slavery.[38]

What this example shows is how many of the things we take for granted in the Church have been and continue to be filtered through the lens of whiteness and white comfort.

---

[37]. Katie Walker Grimes, *Fugitive Saints: Catholicism and the Politics of Slavery* (Minneapolis: Fortress Press, 2017), xiii.

[38]. Grimes, *Fugitive Saints*, xiii–xiv.

As we have already seen, "whiteness" is more than just color, whether that of one's perceived skin tone or of the paint used to depict angels and saints in church art. It is also about power and control, dominance and success, privilege and comfort. Such is the case in the framing of the stories we tell about some of the saints. And yet, there are other ways in which the pervasive whiteness of the American Church is manifested, including who holds power and exercises authority in the Church. Take, for example, the demographic composition of the Church's hierarchical leadership in the United States. Even recently, according to US Conference of Catholic Bishops data in the summer of 2020, there are approximately 37,302 ministerial priests in the United States, and of that number only 250 are identified as African American. That means that African American priests account for 0.7 percent of the total number of US priests, a startling statistic that further reveals the hegemony of white experience, perspective, and culture in ecclesiastical leadership at the parish, diocesan, and national levels. Similarly, at the level of bishops, of the 427 active and retired American bishops only 13 are listed as being of African descent.

The near-universal composition of white clergy and bishops making decisions and providing leadership for the Church in the United States neither reflects a proportionate representation of the ever-growing Catholic population of color in the United States, nor does it naturally allow for the self-criticality needed to become aware of the complexity and pervasiveness of systemic racism and white privilege in the Church. Like all white people in the American context, the white priests and bishops entrusted with ministerial leadership in the Church benefit from the very same unjust structures that simultaneously disadvantage people of color—clergy, religious, and laity alike. So it is not surprising that the statements and policies that American bishops promulgate and the local-level practices of overwhelmingly white clergy fail regularly to register the unacknowledged whiteness of the Church. We will examine this more closely in the next chapter.

Finally, the systemic, structural, and institutional racism of the Catholic Church as a reflection of the broader context in which the Church exists, as well as the explicit embrace and protection of whiteness as normative within the Church, have led to the denial and erasure of Black Catholic history. Because of the ubiquity of white normativity presented in the Church, many white Catholics are surprised to learn that there have been Black Catholics in America for as long as there have been Catholics and people of African descent on this continent. The late Benedictine monk and historian Cyprian Davis, O.S.B., spent his life researching, writing, and teaching about the underappreciated realities of Black Catholics. He has provided historical documentation of Black Catholicism in the United States, authoring the magisterial 1990 book, *The History of Black Catholics in the United States*.[39] In his preface, Davis writes: "Too often the presence of black Catholics through the centuries has been a muted one, a silent witness, an unspoken testimony."[40] This muted, silent, unspoken witness spans the entire history of Christianity, dating back to our faith tradition's Middle Eastern and African origins.

The denial and erasure of a deep and long history of African American Catholic life and worship have been occasioned both by acts of overt racial injustice and as a consequence of negligence arising from the Church's embrace and perpetuation

---

[39]. Cyprian Davis, *The History of Black Catholics in the United States* (New York: Crossroad, 1990).

[40]. Davis, *History of Black Catholics in the United States*, x.

of white normativity.[41] In the case of racial injustice, this is a history marked by chattel slavery, segregation, and white resistance to integration at all levels, from schools to churches.[42] Other overt instances of racial injustice and animus are seen in the prohibition of women and men of color from entrance into the ranks of religious life and ordained ministry.[43] The racism of the Church as institution is more than the sum of individual acts of racist violence and discrimination; it has pervaded all aspects of the Church's life, including who, how, and when people of color were and are admitted to the sacraments.[44]

Despite racial stereotypes that presuppose Black Catholics are largely "converts" to Catholicism from other Christian denominations or religious traditions, there has been and

---

41. For example, see Kim R. Harris, "Black Lives Matter in the Worshipping Church," *National Catholic Reporter*, July 10, 2020. https://www.ncronline.org/news/opinion/black-lives-matter-worshipping-church.

42. For an example of 1960s active white racist rejection of integration efforts in the "northern" city of Chicago, see Matthew J. Cressler, "'Real Good and Sincere Catholics': White Catholicism and Massive Resistance to Desegregation in Chicago, 1965–1968," *Religion and American Culture*, July 29, 2020 (print edition forthcoming), https://doi.org/10.1017/rac.2020.7. See also Matthew J. Cressler, *Authentically Black and Truly Catholic: The Rise of Black Catholicism in the Great Migration* (New York: New York University Press, 2017).

43. See Davis, *History of Black Catholics in the United States*, 98–115, 145–62. See also Caroline Hemesath, *From Slave to Priest: The Inspirational Story of Father Augustine Tolton (1854–1897)* (San Francisco: Ignatius Press, 1973); C. Vanessa White, "Augustus Tolton: Pioneer Pastor," *U.S. Catholic*, February 2014, 55–56; and Shannen Dee Williams, "Subversive Images and Forgotten Truths: A Selected Visual History of Black Women Religious," *American Catholic Studies* 127 (2016): 14–21.

44. See Katie Walker Grimes, *Christ Divided: Antiblackness as Corporate Vice* (Minneapolis: Fortress Press, 2017), 189–222.

continues to be a large and vibrant community of Black Catholics in the United States, often situated in major metropolitan centers, including Chicago, New York, Washington, DC, and southern Louisiana, among others.[45] (Not to mention that the majority of the world's Catholic population exists and is growing in the Global South, which is overwhelmingly composed of people of color.) The very existence of a long-standing, centuries-old Black Catholic community presumed by whites to be composed of "converts" reflects again the operative presumption of white normativity. As Massingale noted earlier, if "Catholic" means "white," then the existence of *Black Catholics* must be—to the white imagination—an anomaly of some kind. This is a clear example of the persistence of systemic racism in the Catholic Church of the United States. In the next chapter, we will look at the statements and teachings that Church leaders have provided on the subject of racism, which, especially in the American context, reveal why little has changed in awakening white Catholics to the realities of systemic racism and white privilege in the Church and broader world.

Further Reading

- Michelle Alexander, *The New Jim Crow: Mass Incarceration in the Age of Colorblindness* (New York: New Press, 2010).

---

[45]. Davis, *History of Black Catholics in the United States*, 260. See also Diana L. Hayes and Cyprian Davis, eds., *Taking Down Our Harps: Black Catholics in the United States* (Maryknoll, NY: Orbis Books, 1998); Cecilia A. Moore, C. Vanessa White, and Paul M. Marshall, eds., *Songs of Our Hearts, Meditations of Our Souls: Prayers for Black Catholics* (Cincinnati: Franciscan Media, 2007); and Darren W. Davis and Donald B. Pope-Davis, *Perseverance in the Parish? Religious Attitudes from a Black Catholic Perspective* (New York: Cambridge University Press, 2017).

- Eduardo Bonilla-Silva, *Racism without Racists: Color-Blind Racism and the Persistence of Racial Inequality in America*, 5th ed. (Lanham, MD: Rowman & Littlefield, 2018).
- Laurie M. Cassidy and Alex Mikulich, eds., *Interrupting White Privilege: Catholic Theologians Break the Silence* (Maryknoll, NY: Orbis Books, 2007).
- M. Shawn Copeland, "White Supremacy and Anti-Black Logics in the Making of U.S. Catholicism," in *Anti-Blackness and Christian Ethics*, ed. Vincent W. Lloyd and Andrew Prevot (Maryknoll, NY: Orbis Books, 2017), 61–76.
- Matthew J. Cressler, *Authentically Black and Truly Catholic: The Rise of Black Catholicism in the Great Migration* (New York: New York University Press, 2017).
- Cyprian Davis, *The History of Black Catholics in the United States* (New York: Crossroad, 1990).
- Darren W. Davis and Donald B. Pope-Davis, *Perseverance in the Parish? Religious Attitudes from a Black Catholic Perspective* (New York: Cambridge University Press, 2017).
- Joe R. Feagin, *The White Racial Frame: Centuries of Racial Framing and Counter-Framing*, 3rd ed. (New York: Routledge, 2020).
- Katie Walker Grimes, *Fugitive Saints: Catholicism and the Politics of Slavery* (Minneapolis: Fortress Press, 2017).
- Diana L. Hayes and Cyprian Davis, eds., *Taking Down Our Harps: Black Catholics in the United States* (Maryknoll, NY: Orbis Books, 1998).
- Bryan N. Massingale, *Racial Justice and the Catholic Church* (Maryknoll, NY: Orbis Books, 2010).
- Alex Mikulich, Laurie Cassidy, and Margaret Pfeil, *The Scandal of White Complicity in US Hyper-Incarceration: A Nonviolent Spirituality of White Resistance* (New York: Palgrave Macmillan, 2013).

- Cecilia A. Moore, C. Vanessa White, and Paul M. Marshall, eds., *Songs of Our Hearts, Meditations of Our Souls: Prayers for Black Catholics* (Cincinnati: Franciscan Media, 2007).
- Khalil Gibran Muhammad, *The Condemnation of Blackness: Race, Crime, and the Making of Modern Urban America* (Cambridge, MA: Harvard University Press, 2010).
- Doris Marie Provine, *Unequal under Law: Race in the War on Drugs* (Chicago: University of Chicago Press, 2007).
- Richard Rothstein, *The Color of Law: A Forgotten History of How Our Government Segregated America* (New York: W. W. Norton, 2017).

5

What Does the Catholic Church Teach about Racism?

Like most things Catholic, the question "What does the Church teach about *racism?*" is not easily answered because there are many layers and levels of official Church teaching. Despite public perceptions of Catholicism as a singular religious institution, a kind of Christian IBM corporation with a CEO (the pope), middle managers (the bishops), customer service representatives (the priests and religious), and customers (the laity), the Catholic Church does not actually operate in this way. It is, as one influential theologian accurately describes it, "a communion of communions."[1] The Church is structured such that it is supposed to operate primarily at the local, diocesan level. This is a reflection of the principle known as subsidiarity, which is one of the key pillars of Catholic social teaching and refers to the idea that organization and governance should be handled by the most immediate or most local competent authority. The officeholder with the highest authority in a given region of the world is the local bishop, who can exercise ordinary

---

[1.] See Jean-Marie-Roger Tillard, *Church of Churches: The Ecclesiology of Communion*, trans. R. C. De Peaux (Collegeville, MN: Liturgical Press, 1992).

magisterium—teaching and pastoral authority—for the diocese he serves as bishop. The pope, who is first and foremost the bishop of the Diocese of Rome, has a distinctive charism and responsibility as the first among equals in the worldwide college of bishops. For this reason, the pope can exercise ordinary magisterium not only for the Church in Rome but also for the entire People of God across the world.[2]

Given that there are thousands of dioceses and therefore thousands of bishops, each of whom is supposed to address the "signs of the times in the light of the gospel" (*Gaudium et Spes*) in each of their local churches,[3] there is a predictable diversity of Church teachings on the subject of racism and racial justice. Understandably, each local bishop and regional conference of bishops ought to take into consideration the particular needs, challenges, and opportunities present in their respective locale when drafting a statement or providing instruction on a moral issue such as racial justice. For that reason, this chapter cannot provide an exhaustive summary or analysis of the manifold responses to racism around the globe. As has been stated throughout this book so far, the primary focus here is the Catholic Church in the United States, which will guide the content and scope of what follows in this chapter.

But because the pope can exercise universal magisterium with authority applying to Catholics in all dioceses, it is important at least to survey some of what has been taught at that international level in the form of papal promulgations as well

---

2. For more, see Richard R. Gaillardetz, *By What Authority? Foundations for Understanding Authority in the Church*, 2nd ed. (Collegeville, MN: Liturgical Press, 2018).

3. Second Vatican Council, *Gaudium et Spes*, 1965, no. 75, http://www.vatican.va/archive/hist_councils/ii_vatican_council/documents/vat-ii_const_19651207_gaudium-et-spes_en.html.

as the universal teaching of the Second Vatican Council. Additionally, there have been some good resources that have been published by Church leaders and conferences of bishops in other parts of the world that offer challenge and inspiration for those of us in the American context; therefore, we will take a brief look at some of these global perspectives. Sadly, the bishops in the United States have not been as proactive or seemingly open to engaging the full complexity of racism and white privilege as they should be. As Bryan Massingale succinctly stated, "Perhaps the most remarkable thing to note concerning U.S. Catholic social teaching on racism is how little there is to note."[4] We will examine what the American bishops have done and what they have failed to do in addressing the issues of racism and privilege. This section of the chapter offers some critical insight into the inadequacies of both the statements about and the implementation of efforts toward racial justice in the American Church with an aim of helping to draw attention to areas in need of improvement. Finally, we will consider some proposals to assist the Church and its leaders in forging a better response to the evils of racism and white supremacy moving forward.

Vatican II and Papal Teaching

Second Vatican Council

The starting point for any examination of the Church's modern teaching on racism is the Second Vatican Council (1962–1965). An ecumenical council such as this is a gathering of all the world's bishops under the authority of the pope, who collectively

---

[4]. Bryan N. Massingale, *Racial Justice and the Catholic Church* (Maryknoll, NY: Orbis Books, 2010), 43.

study, discuss, debate, and approve teaching for the universal Church. Though there have been fewer than two dozen such councils over the Church's two-thousand-year-old history, these solemn gatherings represent the highest teaching authority in the Church. One of the most significant documents of Vatican II is its *Pastoral Constitution on the Church in the Modern World*, known by its Latin title, *Gaudium et Spes*.[5] Among the key themes addressed in this important teaching document is the inalienable dignity and value of the human person. It is within this context that we read: "With respect to the fundamental rights of the person, every type of discrimination, whether social or cultural, whether based on sex, race, color, social condition, language or religion, is to be overcome and eradicated as contrary to God's intent."[6] The language of the prohibition on discrimination is intentionally vague given the global audience of the text, only stating that among other human characteristics, race can never be used as justification for prejudicial action or views. There is also acknowledgment in this section that this fight against discrimination is an ongoing effort: "For in truth it must still be regretted that fundamental personal rights are still not being universally honored."[7]

Pope Pius XI

Vatican II's engagement with the subject of race and racism is far less explicit than that of Pope Pius XI nearly thirty years earlier in his 1937 encyclical letter addressing the political situation in Germany during the rise of the Nazi Party. The pope wrote:

[5.] All Vatican documents are available at www.vatican.va in a variety of modern languages.

[6.] Second Vatican Council, *Gaudium et Spes*, no. 29.

[7.] Second Vatican Council, *Gaudium et Spes*, no. 29.

> Whoever exalts race, or the people, or the State, or a particular form of State, or the depositories of power, or any other fundamental value of the human community—however necessary and honorable be their function in worldly things—whoever raises these notions above their standard value and divinizes them to an idolatrous level, distorts and perverts an order of the world planned and created by God; he is far from the true faith in God and from the concept of life which that faith upholds.[8]

Pius XI goes to great lengths to explicitly reject the discrimination emerging in Germany during the rise of the Third Reich, a discrimination focused primarily at the Jewish people, but also deployed against others whom the Nazis viewed as "less than human" or otherwise "inferior" on the basis of race, religion, and social status, among other characteristics.

Pope John Paul II

In 1988, after a visit to South Africa, Pope John Paul II returned to Rome and directed the Church's Pontifical Council for Justice and Peace to write a lengthy document on the subject of racism. Moved and disturbed as he had been by witnessing the ongoing horrors of racial apartheid in South Africa, as well as by his familiarity with persistent systemic racism in other parts of the world including the United States, John Paul II believed concerted effort was needed to name and respond to the structural injustice present in the Church and world. At the outset of the second section of the document titled "The Church and Racism: Toward a More Fraternal

---

[8]. Pius XI, *Mit Brennender Sorge*, 1937, no. 8.

Society," we read in no uncertain terms: "Today racism has not disappeared. There are even troubling new manifestations of it here and there in various forms, be they spontaneous, officially tolerated or institutionalized."[9] In a move uncommon for official Vatican documents, it names South Africa explicitly and situates the apartheid regime within a broader global history of racism, from genocide of Indigenous peoples to the Atlantic slave trade to Nazi Germany to other contemporary instances of social and civil injustice on the basis of race. The document contrasts these terrible realities with the vision for human dignity, equality, and fraternity (brotherhood and sisterhood) that the Old and New Testaments present as God's intention for human society.

The 1988 document, which was reissued in 2001 as the Vatican's contribution to a conference on racism and intolerance in Durban, South Africa, names the Church's responsibility in responding to racism throughout the world.

> The Church has the sublime vocation of realizing, first of all within herself, the unity of humankind over and above any ethnic, cultural, national, social or other divisions in order to signify precisely that such divisions are now obsolete, having been abolished by the cross of Christ. In doing this, the Church contributes toward promoting the fraternal coexistence of all peoples. . . . It is important that Christians become more aware that they are all called to be a sign in the world. Should they banish all forms of racial, ethnic, national or cultural discrimination from their conduct, the world would recognize better the

---

[9]. Pontifical Council for Justice and Peace, "The Church and Racism: Toward a More Fraternal Society," 1988, no. 8.

newness of the Gospel of reconciliation in the Church, they must anticipate the eschatological and definitive community of the kingdom of God.[10]

The document makes clear that—based on the Church's long-standing tradition of teaching the universal and inalienable dignity and value of every human person, without qualification—no human group "can boast of having a natural superiority over others, or of exercising any discrimination that affects the basic rights of the person."[11]

This document is an extraordinary text, one that does not shy away from the realities and consequences of individual and systemic racism, while also stating overtly that Christians have a divinely mandated responsibility to fight against such discrimination in all forms. The fourth part of the document outlines the manifold ways in which particular Christians and the Church as a whole can aid in the work of racial justice. It calls not only for individual conversion or "change of heart" but also for the difficult work of shedding light on truth and striving toward authentic reconciliation. While a document of great worth and challenging teaching, it nevertheless falls short of explicitly acknowledging the Catholic Church's own complicity in the perpetuation of racial injustice as an institution, which we examined in the previous chapter. Instead, it places the blame on the individual Christians and groups of Christians who make up the Church, as if the two can be distinguishable. Though less egregious in tone and scope, there is a tacit "bad

---

[10]. Pontifical Council for Justice and Peace, "The Church and Racism," no. 22.

[11]. Pontifical Council for Justice and Peace, "The Church and Racism," no. 23.

apples" argument presumed in the document—namely, that to the extent that one can identify racism or racial injustice in the Church, it is on account of some racist individuals who happen to be a part of the Church. Positively, the document concludes with an exhortation for Catholics to respond directly to the persistence of racial injustice in all its forms, pledging that the "Catholic Church encourages all these efforts."[12]

John Paul II also spoke out against racism in a personal manner. He did this during a pastoral visit to the United States in 1999, during which he warned in an address in St. Louis that "there remains another great challenge facing this community ... to put an end to every form of racism," which he described as "a plague" and "one of the most persistent and destructive evils of the nation."[13] Two years later in August 2001, this time in Rome, he dedicated one of his Sunday Angelus addresses to the theme of racism ahead of the United Nations conference in South Africa on racial injustice and xenophobia. Recognizing the increase of racist ideology and behavior around the globe, the pope remarked:

> In the last decades, characterized by the phenomenon of globalization and marked by the worrying resurgence of aggressive nationalism, ethnic violence and widespread phenomena of racial discrimination, human dignity has often been seriously threatened. Every upright conscience cannot but decisively condemn any racism, no matter in what heart or place it is found. Unfortunately it emerges in ever new and unexpected ways, offending

---

[12]. Pontifical Council for Justice and Peace, "The Church and Racism," no. 33.

[13]. John Paul II, "Homily in the Trans World Dome," *Origins* 28 (February 11, 1999): 601.

and degrading the human family. Racism is a sin that constitutes a serious offence against God. The Second Vatican Council reminds us that "We cannot truly pray to God the Father of all if we treat any people in other than brotherly fashion, for all men are created in the image of God. . . . Therefore, the Church reproves, as foreign to the will of Christ, any discrimination against people or any persecution of them on the basis of their race, color, social condition or religion" (*Nostra aetate*, n. 5).[14]

Again, for all the powerful criticism of the cultures of racism present around the world, there is little self-criticality about the inherent racism present *ecclesia ad intra* (within the Church itself). With the Catholic Church's half-millennium history of white and European-centered thinking and colonization across the Western Hemisphere and elsewhere, the Church has played both an overt and at times tacit role in the maintenance of white normativity and attitude of white supremacy.

Pope Benedict XVI

Pope Benedict XVI was less explicit in his critiques of racism in his magisterial texts. Undoubtedly, the pope emeritus affirms the teachings of Vatican II, the work of the Pontifical Council for Justice and Peace, and the insights of his predecessor Pope John Paul II. However, rather than take racism and racial injustice on as a discrete theme, Benedict XVI tended to speak more broadly about the need for solidarity and our obligation to contribute to

---

14. John Paul II, "Angelus," August 26, 2001, http://www.vatican.va/content/john-paul-ii/en/angelus/2001/documents/hf_jp-ii_ang_20010826.html.

the communion of the whole human family. He did this from the outset of his pontificate by linking Christian love of God with love of neighbor as one and the same reality. In his first encyclical letter, *Deus Caritas Est* (*God Is Love*), he wrote: "Love of God and love of neighbor have become one: in the least of the brethren we find Jesus himself, and in Jesus we find God."[15]

One time when Benedict XVI explicitly engaged the subject of racism was on August 17, 2008, almost seven years to the day after his predecessor spoke about the evils of racism in a similar Angelus address. Benedict XVI said:

> How important it is, especially in our time, that every Christian community increasingly deepens its awareness of this in order also to help civil society overcome every possible temptation to give into racism, intolerance and exclusion and to make decisions that respect the dignity of every human being! One of humanity's great achievements is in fact its triumph over racism. However, unfortunately disturbing new forms of racism are being manifested in various Countries. They are often related to social and economic problems which can, however, never justify contempt and racial discrimination. Let us pray that respect for every person everywhere will increase, together with a responsible awareness that only in the reciprocal acceptance of one and all is it possible to build a world distinguished by authentic justice and true peace.[16]

---

[15]. Benedict XVI, *Deus Caritas Est*, 2005, no. 15.
[16]. Benedict XVI, "Angelus," August 17, 2008, http://www.vatican.va/content/benedict-xvi/en/angelus/2008/documents/hf_ben-xvi_ang_20080817.html.

Apart from an overly optimistic take on human progress, which Benedict XVI prematurely declares in terms of humanity's "triumph over racism," his short reflection on racism is in keeping with that of Vatican II and previous papal statements.

Pope Francis

More recently, Pope Francis has spoken out publicly on the topics of racism and racial justice. For example, in the wake of the police murder of George Floyd, the unarmed Black man in Minneapolis, Pope Francis addressed those protestors calling out for police reform and racial justice. During one of his general audiences in June 2020, the pope said: "I have witnessed with great concern the disturbing social unrest in your nation in these past days, following the tragic death of Mr. George Floyd. . . . We cannot tolerate or turn a blind eye to racism and exclusion in any form and yet claim to defend the sacredness of every human life."[17] He then expressed his prayerful solidarity with the people of Minneapolis and around the United States, exhorting the faithful to pray for "the repose of the soul of George Floyd and of all those others who have lost their lives as a result of the sin of racism."[18]

Although Pope Francis, like his two immediate predecessors, has not issued any formal magisterial teaching on racism—such as one might expect to find in an encyclical letter or apostolic exhortation—he has been more outspoken in an

---

[17]. Francis, "General Audience," June 3, 2020, https://www.vaticannews.va/en/pope/news/2020-06/pope-francis-usa-george-floyd-protests-no-racism-violence.html.

[18]. Francis, "General Audience," June 3, 2020.

extemporaneous manner about the evils of racism and the persistence of structural injustice. Weeks after naming George Floyd explicitly in his weekly audience, the pope sent a message to a gathering of Catholic journalists in which he encouraged them to assist in the work of overcoming "the diseases of racism, injustice and indifference that disfigure the face of our common family."[19] From the outset of his ministry as bishop of Rome beginning in 2013, Pope Francis has regularly drawn attention to the plight of migrants, refugees, and people of color throughout Europe and North America. For example, in May 2019, the pope issued a message for the World Day of Migrants and Refugees in which he acknowledged the deleterious consequences of being socialized in a systemic racist culture: "But the problem is not that we have doubts and fears. The problem is when they condition our way of thinking and acting to the point of making us intolerant, closed and perhaps even—without realizing it—racist."[20] A year earlier, Pope Francis admonished political leaders around the world who exploit "the fears and objective difficulties of some groups, using illusory promises for shortsighted electoral interests" in explicitly racist and xenophobic ways.[21]

---

[19]. Nicole Winfield, "Pope Urges US Catholic Media to Overcome Racism," Associated Press, June 30, 2020, https://apnews.com/22b59aa9d4eba4cad03bf35b876e1a23.

[20]. "Pope Francis Sounds Alarm as EU Nationalists Win Big," Agence France-Presse, May 27, 2019, https://www.straitstimes.com/world/europe/pope-francis-sounds-racism-alarm-as-eu-nationalists-win-big.

[21]. Linda Bordoni, "Pope Warns against Upsurge in Racism and Intolerance," *Vatican News*, September 20, 2018, https://www.vaticannews.va/en/pope/news/2018-09/pope-francis-racism-conference-human-rights.html.

The Example of the Church in Rome

While the statements by and responses of popes, pontifical offices, and even the Second Vatican Council have been imperfect and could certainly be improved, these are sadly still far ahead of the work done by the collective of American bishops, as we will see later in this chapter. As Massingale notes, "The church of Rome has been more vigilant, solicitous, concerned, and forthright regarding racial injustice and the plight of racial minorities in the United States than have U.S. Catholics and their leaders. Rome has shown a willingness to confront racial inequality in a way that the U.S. church has yet to muster."[22]

Global Perspectives

While the particular histories and contexts of racial injustice vary by location and culture, Catholics in the United States can learn a lot from our sisters and brothers in faith from other parts of the world. Whereas the American bishops have been somewhat reserved in their exercise of ordinary magisterium on issues relating to the evils of racism, other conferences of bishops around the globe have at times been more direct. The number of local and regional episcopal statements from around the world are too numerous to fully examine here; however, it is worth highlighting key insights from a few that resonate well with experiences in the American context.[23]

---

[22]. Massingale, *Racial Justice and the Catholic Church*, 47.

[23]. For an introduction to and survey of more texts from around the world, see Dawn M. Nothwehr, *That They May Be One: Catholic Social Teaching on Racism, Tribalism, and Xenophobia* (Maryknoll, NY: Orbis Books, 2008).

Bishops of India

Given the compelling case made by Isabel Wilkerson in her 2020 book, *Caste: The Origins of Our Discontents*, about how systemic racial injustice in the United States is best understood within the framework of a "caste system," it is not surprising that one of the most powerful Catholic voices on the subject of racism comes from the bishops of India.[24] Wilkerson's argument is that the United States, socially and culturally, operates according to an unspoken and unacknowledged caste system, which places white people at the top ("dominant caste"), Black people at the bottom ("subordinate caste"), and Latinx, Asian, Indigenous, and other groups somewhere in between. What is most helpful about this shift away from a strict binary, "black-and-white" way of thinking toward a more nuanced stratification of injustice in our context is that it helps account for the range of discrimination, prejudice, and presumed hierarchical standing of each person on an arbitrary basis, which in the United States is ordered by phenotype (physical appearance, especially skin color). If, as Wilkerson contends, we live in a centuries-old, unacknowledged caste system, the way that Catholic leaders in India, where their complex caste system has been operative for millennia, have addressed this issue of systemic injustice can be instructive.

In 1982 the Catholic Bishops' Conference of India issued a "Statement on Caste."[25] The brief but poignant statement opens with acknowledgment of the legislative ways that

---

24. Isabel Wilkerson, *Caste: The Origins of Our Discontents* (New York: Random House, 2020).
25. Catholic Bishops' Conference of India, "Statement on Caste," 1982 (Tiruchirapally, India), http://www.dalitchristians.com/Html/CBCI_Tiruchirapally010482.htm.

Indian independence from colonial rule led to a movement seeking justice outside the oppressive caste system. However, the bishops soberly note: "Notwithstanding all these efforts, much yet remains to be done within the Church and outside particularly in the eradication of what is known as the 'caste mentality' which often finds expression in actions that are manifestly unchristian and even affects, in some areas, the sphere of religious practices."[26] What is immediately striking about this key line is twofold: first, the bishops acknowledge that the injustices of the caste system affect not only the civil and social sphere but also the Church; second, the invocation of "caste mentality" describes a socialized condition that is not merely about individual animus, prejudice, or hatred.

Developing this first theme, the Indian bishops talk about the heart and soul of our Catholic faith: participation in the celebration of the Eucharist. Recognizing the inherent connection between what we say we believe in the sacramental presence of Christ in the bread and wine—as well as in the assembled People of God and in the Word of God—and how we live in socially unjust circumstances, the bishops challenge the faithful in India always to bring these two aspects of faith and action together.

> Catholics, in particular, are called to reflect on whether they can meaningfully participate in the Eucharist without repudiating and seriously striving to root out caste prejudices and similar traditions and sentiments both within the Church and outside. It is intolerable that caste should be a determining factor in membership of

---

26. Catholic Bishops' Conference of India, "Statement on Caste."

pastoral or parish councils and other Church associations; and even worse, in ecclesial appointments and posts of responsibility in religious congregations.[27]

While most Americans are unaccustomed to thinking of racial injustice in the United States according to "caste," one only has to substitute the word "caste" with "race" in the paragraph above to see its applicability in our context. Furthermore, the Indian bishops repeatedly recognize that the injustices they are calling out are not merely external to Church life but deeply embedded in the Church and require the same vigilance and commitment to redress. This is summed up powerfully in the closing lines of the statement:

> The issue of caste and its consequent evil effects is not a peripheral one for the Church, or indeed, for society at large. Delay in facing it—or sometimes even a refusal to do so—is more than a question of human rights. It is betrayal of the Christian vocation. We can no longer watch complacently while millions of our brothers and sisters are denied the rights that flow from their dignity as human beings and children of God.[28]

The moral clarity conveyed in this statement is inspiring and challenging. It offers insights into both the ecclesial and social dimensions of systematic injustice and the tireless effort needed to address it.

---

27. Catholic Bishops' Conference of India, "Statement on Caste."
28. Catholic Bishops' Conference of India, "Statement on Caste."

Bishops of South Africa

The Catholic Church in South Africa shares a similar history with the United States in that the predominant system of injustice centers on race. In both countries white people occupy the dominant caste, whereas Black people are viewed and treated subordinately. But unlike the American context, the South African nation attempted a comprehensive truth and reconciliation process to bring to light the particular and collective racial injustices that persisted throughout the racist apartheid system. In this way, South Africa and the Catholic Church within it were forced to grapple, at least in some manner, with the dangerous memory of racial injustice and white supremacy in a concerted effort, the likes of which have never been attempted in the United States.

A decade after the end of apartheid, South African Catholics continued struggling toward integration and racial justice, but faced numerous challenges in the wake of such an atrociously racist history. Laws can change overnight, but ways of thinking, relating, and behaving can rarely keep pace. For this reason, the bishops of Southern Africa issued a pastoral plan in the form of "A Message to All Catholics in Southern Africa" in 2003.[29] The pastoral and practical vision proposed in the document is deliberately set on a theological foundation. Like the statements of Benedict XVI, the message exhorts Christians in Southern Africa to recall God's intention for "one human community in which all find an experience of belonging to the same human family."[30]

---

[29]. See "A Message to All Catholics in Southern Africa," reprinted in Nothwehr, *That They May Be One*, 133–35.

[30]. "A Message to All Catholics in Southern Africa," in Nothwehr, *That They May Be One*, 134.

What is particularly striking is the forthrightness of the bishops in acknowledging the "uneasiness" women and men socialized in such a racist system would inevitably experience when confronted with "difference in cultural and ethnic expressions" from which they were previously segregated.[31] The naming of discomfort and unease is important but has been lacking in the American context—likely in part because of the powerful forces inside and outside the Church that have denied the deep-seated structures of racism and normative white supremacy. It is important because it does not shy away from the difficult work and deliberate attention that must be paid in order for any hope of racial justice to flourish. White Catholics in the United States can take an important cue from our South African sisters and brothers: the work of racial justice is unavoidably demanding and discomfiting, because it requires facing and addressing painful truths that have harmed those put in subordinate castes and benefited those in the dominant one.

Bishops of the United Kingdom

Finally, in our brief world tour of Catholic statements on racial injustice we stop at the United Kingdom. Over the years, the Catholic Bishops' Conference of England and Wales has produced several insightful statements on racial justice, challenged as that nation has been by its long legacy of colonialism and contemporary struggles to embrace its increasingly multicultural society. In 1993 there was an incident that is all too common in the United States, but far less so in places like England. A young Black man named Stephen Lawrence was murdered in London,

---

[31.] "A Message to All Catholics in Southern Africa," in Nothwehr, *That They May Be One*, 135.

and no suspect was ever charged with the crime. Outrage over the apparent lack of police interest or effort to investigate the crime led to an extensive investigation at the behest of the British Parliament. Sir William Macpherson was tasked with leading the investigation, the final report of which came to be associated with his name: "The Macpherson Report."[32] The nearly four-hundred-page report was published in 1999 and outlined extensive evidence of "institutional racism" in multiple government sectors, including within the London Metropolitan Police. In addition to the striking breadth and depth of the response to one unarmed Black man's unsolved murder in London—as opposed to the horrifying frequency with which Black people in the United States routinely face injustice before the law and are, as we have become increasingly aware, disproportionately likely to be murdered at the hands of law enforcement without any such sustained inquiries—what is notable to us is the response of the Catholic Bishops' Conference of England and Wales to the report.

The same year the Macpherson Report was published, the British bishops' Committee for Racial Relations published its own document under the heading "Serving a Multi-Ethnic Society."[33] Opening with a summary remark of Christian mission and a paraphrase of the first lines of Vatican II's *Gaudium et Spes*, the bishops wrote: "The gospel values which underpin our work call us to service all, especially the poor

---

[32.] For the full report, see "The Stephen Lawrence Inquiry: Report of an Inquiry by Sir William Macpherson of Cluny," February 1999, https://assets.publishing.service.gov.uk/government/uploads/system/uploads/attachment_data/file/277111/4262.pdf.

[33.] Catholic Bishops' Conference of England and Wales, "Serving a Multi-Ethnic Society," April 1999, https://www.carj.org.uk/wp-content/uploads/2020/07/Serving-a-Multiethnic-Society.pdf.

and marginalized."[34] But what is most notable about the tone and engagement of the document is the direct and forthright manner in which the bishops acknowledge that what the Macpherson Report says about civil society and its institutions—namely, the persistence of systemic and "institutional racism"—*also applies to the Church*. The bishops define institutional racism as "a form of structural sin and primarily a sin of omission" and then state: "Knowing that institutional racism exists in some of the key institutions of our society, we cannot assume that Catholic organizations and institutions are unaffected. In such a situation, we become culpable if we fail to take stock and examine carefully the nature of the service we offer."[35] The rest of the document focuses on how each of the Catholic institutions in England and Wales are to undergo a thorough review to see the ways in which their work, structure, and ministry have been affected by the reality of institutional racism and are to work to remedy such racial injustice.

The British bishops take seriously the Church's teaching on structural sin and situate an otherwise secular report within the context of orthodox Catholic teaching on the nature of sin and social justice. Not only do they apply this Christian analysis to the broader social context of Great Britain but they also apply it to themselves and the institutions that operate and minister under the banner of Catholicism in England. There is recognition on their part in this document that the continued validity of their moral authority necessitates such introspection and critical examination in order to authentically carry out the

---

34. Catholic Bishops' Conference of England and Wales, "Serving a Multi-Ethnic Society."

35. Catholic Bishops' Conference of England and Wales, "Serving a Multi-Ethnic Society."

work of the gospel. Sadly, as we shall see in the next section of this chapter, the same cannot generally be said about their American counterparts. While there are dozens of other instances of insightful and challenging statements and teaching documents from around the globe, these three from India, South Africa, and England offer us a sampling and a model for how Catholics in the United States might think about responding to racial injustice in the Church and world.

Statements from the United States Conference of Catholic Bishops

Over the course of the last century the bishops of the United States have published four documents that focused on race and racial justice.

"Discrimination and Christian Conscience" (1958)

The first was released in 1958, four years after the historic *Brown v. Board of Education* decision, which was the United States Supreme Court ruling that finally rejected the long-standing legalized segregation of the Jim Crow era. In the wake of this significant court ruling, there was pressure placed on the American bishops from Pope Pius XII and other Church leaders from outside the country who were appalled at the racial injustice plaguing the United States.[36] Despite the resistance on the part of the American hierarchy to speak out boldly and publicly about racial injustice, the short final document, titled

---

36. See Massignale, *Racial Justice and the Catholic Church*, 53–55; John F. Cronin, "Religion and Race," *America*, June 23–30, 1984; and William Osborne, *The Segregated Covenant: Race Relations and American Catholics* (New York: Herder & Herder, 1967).

"Discrimination and Christian Conscience,"[37] contains several notable elements.

The statement acknowledges the moral and doctrinal foundations for why legally enforced segregation is unacceptable from a Catholic perspective. The reasons outlined range from the natural moral law, which enshrines the universal dignity of all human beings, to those more overtly Christian reasons such as the universality of Christ's saving life, death, and resurrection. The primary aim of this document was to outline the Catholic case against racial segregation; therefore, it does not offer as comprehensive a vision about the evils of systemic racism and white supremacy as we might have wished. Nevertheless, the bishops express a twofold reason for unequivocal Catholic opposition to racial segregation: that the discriminatory laws of the United States have failed in both theory and practice. In theory, the legal justification for Jim Crow segregation was "separate but equal," to which the bishops responded that the theory was always flawed. By virtue of the imposed separation, one group of people was already placed in a social position of inferiority. In practice, the premise of "equality" never existed. The statement explains: "It is a matter of historical fact that segregation in our country has led to oppressive conditions and the denial of basic human rights for the Negro. This is evident in the fundamental fields of education, job opportunity, and housing."[38]

For its apparent directness on the subject of segregation's inherent sinfulness, the statement applies the proverbial "foot on

---

[37]. National Conference of Catholic Bishops (NCCB), "Discrimination and Christian Conscience," 1958, https://www.usccb.org/issues-and-action/cultural-diversity/african-american/resources/upload/Discrimination-Christian-Conscience-Nov-14-1958.pdf.

[38]. NCCB, "Discrimination and Christian Conscience," no. 16.

the brakes" in its conclusion, exhorting caution and "prudence" as if to dissuade Catholics from the urgency of the moment. Additionally, beyond the "let's take it easy" approach of the bishops present in the text, the statement lacks any concrete direction or proposals for social or ecclesial changes. As Massingale explains, "Clearly the bishops had no intention of making this document a bold clarion call to action. Catholics were not being urged to become proactive agents of racial justice. Rather, the bishops hoped that the faithful would 'seize the mantle of leadership from both the agitator and the racist.'"[39]

In truth, the 1958 document had little practical effect or consequence in the ecclesial or social spheres, which is something that the bishops of the United States were forced to acknowledge a decade later when they issued their next document on race in 1968. In the opening section of the new text, titled "Statement on National Race Crisis,"[40] the bishops acknowledge the earlier statement and how it "condemned racism in all its forms," but also recognized that "now—ten years later—it is evident that we did not do enough; we have much more to do."[41]

"Statement on National Race Crisis" (1968)

One can read the 1968 statement as a complement to the 1958 document. Whereas the 1958 text offered explicit theological and moral reasons for the evils of racism and segregation but lacked concrete suggestions for action or change, the 1968

---

[39]. Massingale, *Racial Justice and the Catholic Church*, 53.

[40]. National Conference of Catholic Bishops (NCCB), "Statement on National Race Crisis," 1968, https://www.usccb.org/issues-and-action/cultural-diversity/african-american/resources/upload/Statement-on-National-Race-Crisis-April-25-1968.pdf.

[41]. NCCB, "Statement on National Race Crisis," nos. 1 and 4.

text provides more concrete recommendations for the Church and its members but lacks a robust theological grounding for the claims. Two of the most significant developments we see center on the bishops' explicit acknowledgment of institutional racism (vs. the more colloquial view that racism is merely about individual actors) and their recognition of racism *within* the Catholic Church (vs. merely an external or societal issue). These are no small admissions. In the wake of a tumultuous decade, which included widespread civil rights activism, the assassination of an American president and key civil rights leaders, and overt instances of racist violence and discrimination, the bishops appear to have felt compelled in a way previously unseen. This is something that Massingale has noted throughout his analysis of these and other documents from American Church leaders on racial justice. He explains that, in the case of the 1958 and 1968 documents, "it took a strong external stimulus in the form of several urgent social and ecclesial crises to compel the bishops to act." He adds: "My studies thus far lead me to believe that the U.S. bishops act corporately on racism only in response to external pressure from Rome and/or grave crises in church or society."[42]

In the two documents issued during the decade marking the height of the American civil rights movement and the crises of racial injustice that spurred on such social action, we see some fundamental principles laid out in the form of the ordinary magisterial teaching of the bishops. These pastoral letters admonish the faithful to take seriously the realities of racial injustice present in society and the Church, not just as some kind of external political concern but as something that is inextricably tied to the doctrinal and moral foundations of

---

42. Massingale, *Racial Justice and the Catholic Church*, 61.

Christian life. Despite these efforts, imperfect as they may have been in their own time, it would appear that few Catholics—clergy and laity—ever read or took seriously these pastoral documents. As a result, little change took hold and little progress in the Catholic approach to racism and racial justice ensued.

"Brothers and Sisters to Us" (1979)

More than a decade had passed since the promulgation of the "Statement on National Race Crisis" when the United States bishops published their third pastoral letter on racism in 1979, this time with the revealing title "Brothers and Sisters to Us."[43] The title is telling because of what is unwittingly conveyed about the authorship and presumed audience of the text. Before reading the document itself, which has many important and strong points, the title signals that the composers of the text—written on behalf of an overwhelmingly white group of bishops—presume a certain white normativity in Catholicism (or at least in the Catholicism of the United States). The implication of the title is that Black Catholics are somehow still "other" because they, while brothers and sisters in Christ, are still somehow removed from the authorial "us" (i.e., white Catholics). While the title is regrettable, the document itself is perhaps the strongest of the four the United States bishops have released.

The bishops situate the 1979 statement within the trajectory of the two previous documents, noting that many of the social and ecclesial ills of racial injustice that prompted the earlier statements still persist. The pastoral letter also states clearly,

---

43. United States Conference of Catholic Bishops (USCCB), "Brothers and Sisters to Us," 1979, https://www.usccb.org/committees/african-american-affairs/brothers-and-sisters-us.

"Racism is an evil which endures in our society and in our Church," naming racism as a problem internally for the Church as much as it is a problem externally.[44] One of the most notable lines of argument throughout this document is the admittance of systemic and institutional racism.

> The structures of our society are subtly racist, for these structures reflect the values which society upholds. They are geared to the success of the majority and the failure of the minority. Members of both groups give unwitting approval by accepting things as they are. Perhaps no single individual is to blame. The sinfulness is often anonymous but nonetheless real. The sin is social in nature in that each of us, in varying degrees, is responsible. All of us in some measure are accomplices.[45]

The 1979 document offers the most thorough engagement with the complex realities of racism in the American context, not shying away from the "evils of the past" or the ways in which "racism itself persists in covert ways" today. The statement acknowledges the transformation of the American culture of racism as it takes new and often "hidden" forms in the modern context of the post–civil rights movement era.

The document also names the Church's complicity in the persistence of structures of racism, in terms of both individual culpability and that of the Church as an institution.

> How great, therefore, is that sin of racism which weakens the Church's witness as the universal sign of unity among all peoples! How great the scandal given by racist

---

44. USCCB, "Brothers and Sisters to Us."
45. USCCB, "Brothers and Sisters to Us."

Catholics who make the Body of Christ, the Church, a sign of racial oppression! Yet all too often the Church in our country has been for many a "white Church," a racist institution.

Each of us as Catholics must acknowledge a share in the mistakes and sins of the past. Many of us have been prisoners of fear and prejudice. We have preached the Gospel while closing our eyes to the racism it condemns. We have allowed conformity to social pressures to replace compliance with social justice.[46]

In addition to other meritorious aspects of "Brothers and Sisters to Us," the document emphasizes a theme central to Martin Luther King Jr.'s own civil rights advocacy but one that is often overlooked or dismissed by whites—namely, the intersection of racism and poverty. The 1979 document connects the economic and social injustices that hold back entire communities of people on the basis of race, whether in terms of housing or job access.

As if to bring together the best elements of the two predecessor texts, the 1979 document presents *both* doctrinal and moral foundations for the Christian imperative to respond to the sin of racism *and* concrete suggestions for action in the Church and society. As Massingale summarizes, "Thus *Brothers and Sisters to Us* is a strongly worded document that forcefully and unequivocally condemns racism in its contemporary manifestations as an evil and a sin. As such, it offered great promise of a new beginning in the Catholic story of race relations."[47] But, as Massingale and many other observers have concluded, it was a promise of a new beginning that went unfulfilled for many of the same reasons the two previous documents were ineffective.

[46.] USCCB, "Brothers and Sisters to Us."
[47.] Massingale, *Racial Justice and the Catholic Church*, 67.

The primary reason had to do with lack of attention to the teaching and the absence of the individual and collective will to change a long-standing pattern of white normativity and institutional racism in the Church. On the twenty-fifth anniversary of the document's publication, the United States bishops released a study on the state of the question, which presented a bleak picture of the document's minimal impact.[48] Among the many indictments of omission, neglect, and indifference in the face of the pastoral teachings on racism in the American Church, the report concluded that the "Church's statements condemning racism have not had their intended effect of reducing the pervasiveness of racist attitudes over the last twenty-five years."[49] It would be another fourteen years before another document on racism would be published by the USCCB, making it a total of thirty-nine years since the last official pastoral statement was released on the subject. And this 2018 document would prove to be, in many ways, the least effective of the four.

"Open Wide Our Hearts" (2018)

In the four decades since the American bishops last released a statement on racism, Catholic theologians, pastors, and activists had eagerly awaited an updating—an *aggiornamento*, to use the Italian term applied to Vatican II—of the Church's local teaching on this personal and systemic evil. The document, titled "Open Wide Our Hearts: The Enduring Call to Love—A Pastoral

---

[48.] See USCCB, "We Walk by Faith and Not by Sight: The Church's Response to Racism in the Years following 'Brothers and Sisters to Us'" (Washington, DC: USCCB Publications, 2004).

[49.] As quoted in Massingale, *Racial Justice and the Catholic Church*, 70.

Letter Against Racism,"[50] was overwhelmingly approved by the American bishops during their November 2018 meeting. While nearly a half century is a long time to wait for a new statement on a persistent social and ecclesial evil, regardless of historical circumstances, the events in the United States since the 2016 presidential election only increased the need for a new pastoral letter. The rise in explicit racist behavior and hate crimes since the election of President Donald Trump, the overt support of his administration's policies by white supremacists and extremist groups, the anti-migrant rhetoric associated with the building of a southern border wall, and the unabashed refusal to condemn Nazi and white supremacist groups after the 2017 incidents in Charlottesville, Virginia, had only heightened the sense of urgency that the American bishops needed to exercise their teaching authority on this topic.

At first glance, "Open Wide Our Hearts" appears in keeping with its three predecessors. Much of what is said is good, if only expressed more timidly than it had been in some of the previous documents. In a way that builds on the 1979 document, the 2018 text acknowledges the reality of systemic racism, but only introduces it pages after first identifying racism as primarily "when—consciously or unconsciously—*a person* holds that his or her own race or ethnicity is superior, and therefore judges persons of other races or ethnicities as inferior or unworthy of equal regard."[51] This is not untrue, but it's far from reflecting the comprehensive nature of systemic racism that precedes and socializes individual prejudice. The emphasis

---

50. United States Conference of Catholic Bishops (USCCB), "Open Wide Our Hearts: The Enduring Call to Love—A Pastoral Letter Against Racism," 2018, https://www.usccb.org/resources/open-wide-our-hearts_0.pdf.

51. USCCB, "Open Wide Our Hearts," 3, emphasis added.

on the personal dimension of racism too easily covers over its communal, structural, institutional, and ecclesial nature. And this prioritization of individual acts of racial animus over the deeply embedded structures of systemic racism in society and the Church is seen throughout the document.

While the new document does attempt to expand the horizon of those who are burdened, oppressed, or otherwise harmed by racism with three short sections dedicated to Native American, African American, and Hispanic experiences, the terms selected and language used here raise some serious questions. In the section on Native Americans, for instance, European colonizers are only referred to tepidly as "explorers, then pioneers" and later as "white European immigrants and pioneers."[52] These descriptions recast colonizers as neutral or even heroic figures without sufficient attention to the imperial and ecclesial motivations, practices, or legacies once these whites arrived from across the Atlantic.

Furthermore, the sentence construction in these sections is notably passive: "African Americans *have been branded*,"[53] "African Americans *were disadvantaged*,"[54] "Hispanics *have been referred to* by countless derogatory names,"[55] and so on. This raises the most glaring issue with the new document. It elicits an uncomfortable question: Branded, disadvantaged, and referred to *by whom?* Who exactly is responsible for the problem of racism? The authors of the document seem to go to great lengths to avoid addressing this question head-on. Readers of the text are led to believe that oppression, subjugation, genocide, chattel

---

52. USCCB, "Open Wide Our Hearts," 10 and 13.
53. USCCB, "Open Wide Our Hearts," 14, emphasis added.
54. USCCB, "Open Wide Our Hearts," 14, emphasis added.
55. USCCB, "Open Wide Our Hearts," 15, emphasis added

slavery, racist violence, unjust legislation, and so on merely befell people of color, as if by chance.

As we have seen throughout this book so far, particularly in chapter 3, the truth is that racism is a *white problem* because in this society white people hold the power, establish the institutions, and set the social norms. The latest USCCB document does not come anywhere close to acknowledging or clearly stating this fact. At least the 1979 document recognized Catholic complicity, if sadly still presupposing white normativity in the Church, and therefore at least held up something of a mirror to white Catholics by challenging them to see their own culpability and role in the persistence of personal and institutional racism.

In this way, the most recent statement from the US bishops on racism appears to go *backward* in its assessment of the "signs of the times." One simple measure of this reactionary shift is in the language that is and isn't used in the document. It is striking that the word "sin" appears at least fourteen times in the document and "racism" more than fifty, but the terms "privilege" and "supremacy" are *never* mentioned. When "white" appears in the body of the text, it is only in reference to historical eras long gone—those "white European immigrants" who arrived to find Native Americans, a white priest who disparaged Fr. Augustus Tolton in the nineteenth century, white parishioners who once upon a time received Communion ahead of Black Catholics in segregated parishes of yesteryear. While the document states that "some have called" racism in the United States "our country's original sin," it nevertheless fails to name the sinner.[56] Whether intended or not, this document does not adequately challenge white Catholics to consider their role in a systemically racist

---

56. USCCB, "Open Wide Our Hearts," 6.

society and Church; it lets whites too easily off the hook by failing to name the other side of the coin of racist oppression: white privilege.

The specter that haunts the latest document is the unacknowledged reality that racism is a white problem and that, while systemic racism affects everybody, it benefits white folk to the disadvantage of people of color. Most people know that overt racial oppression and discrete racist acts are wrong. This is a theme present in all the statements from the American bishops going back to 1958. Another pastoral document to reiterate this point is not needed. Instead, what is needed—but wasn't delivered in this text—is a strong statement with a clear message exhorting those in the position of social and cultural dominance that they must change if there is any hope of a different future. As white Catholics, we need to be challenged more than the teachings by our bishops in the United States have challenged us so far.

Even with its limitations, the current USCCB document might nevertheless spur on substantive discussion, reflection, and action if it were to be taken seriously in all the dioceses of the United States. In November 2019, a year after "Open Wide Our Hearts" was published, journalist Olga Segura contacted all 197 US Catholic dioceses to inquire if and how local churches received the document and put into action new initiatives.[57] While twelve dioceses already had some form of anti-racism programming in place even before the 2018 document, thirty additional dioceses reported that they had started new initiatives.

---

57. Olga Segura, "I Reached Out to Every U.S. Diocese. Here Are the Ones Implementing the 2018 Pastoral Letter on Racism," *America,* November 21, 2019, https://www.americamagazine.org/faith/2019/11/21/i-reached-out-every-us-diocese-here-are-ones-implementing-2018-pastoral-letter.

But that still only represents approximately 21 percent of the total dioceses in the country. One of the more impressive new initiatives came from the Diocese of Houma-Thibodaux, Louisiana, where Bishop Shelton J. Fabre—who also happened to be the chair of the USCCB's Ad Hoc Committee against Racism, which drafted the 2018 document—pledged "to have all seminarians studying in his diocese participate in Xavier University of New Orleans' Summer Institute for Black Catholic Studies."[58] The Institute for Black Catholic Studies (IBCS) was founded in 1980; "conceived in an interdisciplinary context, the various program components of the Institute advance a holistic appreciation of the human person. In critical appropriation of the African heritage of Black Catholics, the Institute is intentionally intergenerational and accords a place of special honor and respect to the Elders of our community," as outlined in the IBCS history.[59] It is a unique program that specializes in the rich tradition of Black Catholicism, features renowned faculty from various academic and pastoral institutions, and is a resource not as well known as it should be.

Unfortunately, as Segura's reporting reflects, the vast majority of American dioceses have yet to actively put the teaching on racism into practice. Part of the problem Segura identifies in her article is the lack of broad consultation by the USCCB's drafting committee, including not consulting many of the faculty at the IBCS and other experts. Furthermore, laity of all racial identities were generally left out of the drafting process, which also helps explain the text's at-times tone-deaf quality and the lack of broader buy-in regarding the document's reception

---

[58]. Segura, "I Reached Out to Every U.S. Diocese." For more information on Xavier University's IBCS, see https://www.xula.edu/ibcs.

[59]. See "History," Xavier University's IBCS, accessed February 4, 2021, https://www.xula.edu/ibcs-history.

in the US Church. One constructive proposal that Segura offers is for Church leaders to embrace Pope Francis's long-standing call for a more synodal Church, which means a Church that engages in dialogue, incorporates the experiences and views of all the faithful, and is open to the movement and guidance of the Holy Spirit. To this end, she suggests a "national synod on racism that would allow us to move past listening sessions and develop ways to concretely implement the action items laid out in 'Open Wide Our Hearts.'"[60] Noting that many of the Church officials and laypeople she spoke with were uncertain about where and how to begin initiatives aimed at anti-racism work in the Church, Segura offered this closing thought: "A synod could help jumpstart the conversation and help local leaders move past listening sessions and create a more responsive church."[61]

People of color are painfully aware of the reality and consequences of systemic racism because they cannot avoid it. However, white people—including white *Catholics*—are, as we've discussed in this book so far, often blissfully unaware of our complicity and role in the very same structures of oppression. That's no accident. Institutions, structures, and policies in this country have been designed (sometimes consciously, sometimes unwittingly) to ensure continued white dominance while also occluding the real dynamics at play. The lack of substantive and direct pastoral documents that address both systemic racism *and* white privilege head-on leaves white Catholics without the loving challenge that authentic Christian faith demands of us. The result is that most whites can feel assured of our morally superior status by limiting how we talk about racism to a few overtly racist "bad apples" in society. Although a serious effect

---

[60]. Segura, "I Reached Out to Every U.S. Diocese."
[61]. Segura, "I Reached Out to Every U.S. Diocese."

of racism has been the internalized oppression experienced by people of color, racism has been and remains a white problem because nothing will change as long as those of us who benefit from an unjust system remain ignorant on the topic. It is not enough for the American Church to decry the sin of racism; we must dare to name the sinner too.

Proposals for Anti-Racist Church Leadership

While the collective responses by the USCCB have left the faithful wanting stronger, clearer, and more prophetic denunciations of the evils of racism and white supremacy as well as acknowledgment of the Church's continued complicity, there have been a handful of individual bishops and religious congregations that have released their own statements on racism and racial justice to varying degrees of thoroughness and effectiveness. Additionally, in 1984 ten Black bishops in the United States coauthored a pastoral letter on evangelization titled "What We Have Seen and Heard," which offers a clear and direct acknowledgment of the persistence and insidiousness of systemic racism in the country and Church.[62] Sadly, this document is not as well known as those documents authored by the USCCB collectively, but it offers a more honest assessment of the challenges of racism in the effort of evangelization and in the broader life of the Church. For example, they write pointedly: "This racism, at once subtle and masked, still festers within our Church as within our society. It is the racism that

---

62. Joseph L. Howze et al., "What We Have Seen and Heard: A Pastoral Letter on Evangelization from the Black Bishops of the United States," September 9, 1984, https://www.usccb.org/issues-and-action/cultural-diversity/african-american/resources/upload/what-we-have-seen-and-heard.pdf.

in our minds remains the major impediment to evangelization within our community."[63]

In 2000 Bryan Massingale published a detailed analysis of what individual American bishops had said publicly on racism during the 1990s, which is an essay worth reading in its entirety.[64] In the two decades since the publication of that article, there have been other statements released under the exercise of individual bishops' ordinary magisterium, which means the statements have authoritative weight in the authoring bishops' respective dioceses. One notable example of a powerful and generally comprehensive statement on racism, which was occasioned by a tragic mass shooting, is that of Bishop Mark Seitz of El Paso, Texas. His pastoral letter, titled "Night Will Be No More," was published in October 2019 and garnered a lot of positive attention for his willingness not only to decry racially motivated violence and racism in general but also to name the reality and persistence of white supremacy in American society.[65] Sadly, Seitz is still an exception to the episcopal rule in the United States.

On the one hand, it is not only up to the bishops to make statements and model behaviors that promote anti-racism and name white supremacy in order to dismantle this evil. It is up to all the baptized, all the faithful who make up the Church, which is the Body of Christ. On the other hand, however, bishops rightly receive the most attention for both their positive and

---

63. Howze et al., "What We Have Seen and Heard," 20.

64. Bryan N. Massingale, "James Cone and Recent Catholic Episcopal Teaching on Racism," *Theological Studies* 61 (2000): 700–730.

65. Mark Seitz, "Night Will Be No More: Pastoral Letter to the People of God in El Paso," October 13, 2019, https://www.hopeborder.org/nightwillbenomore-eng. For analysis, see Daniel P. Horan, "In His Letter on Racism, Seitz Gets Right What US Bishops Got Wrong," *National Catholic Reporter*, October 16, 2019.

their inadequate responses, not because they have some special powers or unique abilities but because they have been entrusted with distinctive responsibilities by virtue of their offices as the primary pastors and teachers of the local church. The office of diocesan bishop is not merely a promotion in rank; it is a real and symbolic responsibility to preserve unity and communion within the local church, and between the local church and universal Church. The failure to take seriously the evil of racism and white supremacy in our society and Church is, therefore, a failure of the episcopal office; it amounts to what we in the Catholic Church call a "sin of omission," or the sin of *not doing* what one *ought to do*. Generally speaking, most episcopal statements on racism state the obvious about the moral evil and sinfulness of individual racist animus in terms of attitudes and behaviors, but rarely delve deep into the systemic, structural, or institutional complexities of the two-sided coin known as racism and white privilege.

Since Christianity is and always has been a religion of conversion and pilgrimage—beginning with Jesus' own selection of disciples who were themselves flawed and "works in progress" (like us) and who were invited to grow into their faith (also like us)—there is always room for improvement and renewed commitment to doing more. With this in mind, I want to close this chapter by reviewing some of the insights Bryan Massingale presents at the conclusion of his analysis of American episcopal statements on racism. Written more than two decades ago, these proposals still offer all of us Catholics—but especially those entrusted with leadership in the Church—guidance on how the Church can better think, pray, reflect, and talk about racism and white privilege.

Massingale proposes "six shifts" to help steer the dominant Catholic response to racism in the American context toward a more holistic and authentic engagement.[66] The first is for Catholics to shift their focus from just "racism" as such to include "white privilege." The logic behind this is readily apparent: nearly everybody agrees that racism, however defined, is a moral evil and sinful. That does not need to be restated ad nauseam as has been the practice of the American bishops since 1958. Despite some individual exceptions to the rule—such as in the cases of Bishop Seitz of El Paso in 2019 and Bishop Edward Braxton in 2015 or that of Cardinal Francis George of Chicago in 2001, Bishop Dale Melczek of Gary in 2003, and Archbishop Alfred Hughes of New Orleans in 2006[67]— the general trend of the American episcopacy has been to focus on what Massingale has called the "commonsense" definition of racism that centers on racially motivated animus. What is lacking is acknowledgment of and engagement with the other side of the coin of racism—namely, white privilege. Racism is not merely about harm done to one group; it is also about how

---

[66]. As should be abundantly apparent throughout this book, I am deeply indebted to the skillful and in-depth research of Fr. Bryan Massingale. For more on his six proposals, see Massingale, "James Cone and Recent Catholic Episcopal Teaching on Racism," 726–29.

[67]. See Seitz, "Night Will Be No More"; Bishop Edward Braxton, "The Racial Divide in the United States: A Reflection for the World Day of Peace 2015," January 1, 2015, https://www.diobelle.org/bishop-emeritus/writings/287-bishop-braxton-writes-a-letter-on-racial-divide-in-the-united-states; Cardinal Francis George, "Dwell in My Love: A Pastoral Letter on Racism," April 4, 2001, https://legacy.archchicago.org/Cardinal/pdf/DwellInMyLove_10thAnniversary.pdf; Bishop Dale Melczek, "Created in God's Image: The Sin of Racism and a Call to Conversion," *Origins* 33 (September 25, 2003): 264–72; and Archbishop Alfred Hughes, "'Made in the Image of God': A Pastoral Letter on Racial Harmony," December 2006, https://files.ecatholic.com/16596/documents/2019/2/Pastoral%20Letter%20of%20Racial%20Harmony%2012162006.pdf?t=1550672452000.

the systems, structures, and institutions that perpetuate that harm on some also benefit others. More has to be said about this to challenge those in what Isabel Wilkerson calls the "dominant caste" of the United States: white people. As we have seen throughout this book, white comfort has typically served as the determining factor in what Church leaders discuss and, equally importantly, *how* it is discussed. Avoidance of speaking about white privilege for fear of upsetting the majority white Catholic population is untenable if racial justice is truly the goal.

Second, Massingale explains that we need to shift our efforts away from toothless exhortations—he uses the technical term "parenesis," from the Greek for "advice" or "counsel"—to more substantive analysis. What this means is that any genuine effort to address racism and white privilege in this country and in our Church requires a social and institutional analysis that will, by its very nature, be both illuminating and discomfiting. It is not enough simply to restate that racially motivated animus and anti-Black prejudice, for example, are sinful and wrong. That does not address the deep-seated socialization of white Catholics in a systemically racist culture, nor does it address the problems of racism and white normativity in the Catholic Church. Those dimensions of the problem require sustained and scientific analysis, which is available in myriad forms but almost never consulted in official Church statements on racism and racial justice.

Third, with an eye toward how we form our consciences, we need to shift our emphasis away from merely "personal sin" to "structures of sin." It is far too easy for individuals, especially white Catholics like me, to hear about the sin of racism as described in a personal sense and conclude that it doesn't involve me because I may not harbor any conscious racially motivated animus. But that does not adequately account for the sinful structures in which all white Catholics are embedded and from which we unwittingly benefit. In order for something to rise to the level of a "personal sin," one has to freely choose to engage in that activity or behavior. However, as Pope John Paul II explained decades ago, there are also structures of sin that must be named, understood, and confronted in order to address the bigger context of sin and evil, which affects us all.[68]

Fourth, when it comes to moral discourse about racism and privilege, the conversation needs to shift away from "tolerance" and "decency" toward "distributive justice." What is meant here is that it is not enough to admonish white Catholics to merely be polite, tolerant, or decent toward BIPOC. As we have seen in the statements by the USCCB, too much of the Catholic conversation about racism has concluded with an exhortation to niceness. But what is not considered frequently enough is the interrelated nature of systemic injustice. This includes the bigger picture of housing, income, health, and class inequality that is tied to the structures of racial injustice in this country. Furthermore, it is worth noting that some anti-racist scholars and activists have rightly called for attention to reparations as a constitutive part of what Catholic ethicists call "distributive justice," which essentially refers to the sharing of the common good among all peoples.[69] Some Catholic organizations have

---

[68]. John Paul II, *Sollicitudo Rei Socialis*, "On the Twentieth Anniversary of *Populorum Progressio*," 1987, http://www.vatican.va/content/john-paul-ii/en/encyclicals/documents/hf_jp-ii_enc_30121987_sollicitudo-rei-socialis.html.

[69]. For example, see Matthew J. Cressler, "What White Catholics Owe Black Americans," *Slate*, September 2, 2016, https://slate.com/news-and-politics/2016/09/georgetowns-reparations-are-to-be-commended-but-catholics-still-owe-black-americans-more.html.

taken up this charge, such as Georgetown University, which has established an educational fund for the descendants of those persons enslaved by the Jesuit community that founded the college.[70]

Fifth, Massingale calls for a "shift from moral suasion to liberating awareness."[71] What he means here is that too much of the American bishops' language is focused on an appeal to conscience and the general structure of authentic Christian discipleship: living the gospels and following the life and teachings of Jesus Christ. The problem with that approach surfaces when you realize that it is a moral appeal to what the faithful are expected to already know and see. And yet, one of the biggest problems for white Catholics is that their very position in a racist society as the unwitting beneficiaries of an unjust system means they are typically shielded from seeing the complexities and nuances of racial injustice, including their own place within it. Therefore, one of the key aims for Catholic leaders in America must be to educate the faithful on precisely these uncomfortable truths and realities from which they have been sheltered. This is what Massingale means by "liberating awareness" because, as Jesus said in John's gospel, "the truth will make you free" (Jn 8:32). But we should steady ourselves

---

70. See Olga Segura, "Georgetown Students Voted to Pay for Reparations. On Juneteenth, the Debate Comes to Congress," *America*, June 19, 2019, https://www.americamagazine.org/politics-society/2019/06/19/georgetown-students-voted-pay-reparations-juneteenth-debate-comes; and Rachel L. Swarns, "Is Georgetown's $400,000-a-Year Plan to Aid Slave Descendants Enough?," *New York Times*, October 30, 2019, https://www.nytimes.com/2019/10/30/us/georgetown-slavery-reparations.html.

71. Massingale, "James Cone and Recent Catholic Episcopal Teaching on Racism," 729.

for the fact that this truth is a hard truth, and while ultimately liberating, it is nevertheless a difficult and often thankless task to help white Catholics become more aware of the reality around us.

Finally, the sixth shift is "from unconscious racial supremacy to intentional racial solidarity."[72] Here Massingale shines a light on one of the most underappreciated but widespread lacunae of formal statements from American bishops on matters of race and racial justice—namely, the unwillingness to engage, study, hear, and learn from women and men of color. When looking over the decades of statements from American bishops, it becomes immediately clear that few, if any, Black Catholics or other Catholics of color were consulted or cited in the drafting of these documents. As Massingale notes, "Reverent listening to the voices of those at the margins—being attentive to their values, fears, hopes, dreams, pain and anger—is often the only way that the authentic demands of justice can become known and the gospel call to conversion can be heard."[73] In recent years, this openness and attentiveness have been rarely demonstrated. One clear exception is Bishop Mark Seitz's 2019 text. However, especially since the American bishops are overwhelmingly white, this shift to solicit and *hear* the voices of those who know firsthand both the suffering on account of systemic racism and the beauty, joy, and gift of Black Catholicism is absolutely essential—not only for the bishops and their supporting staff but for all white Catholics in the United States.

---

72. Massingale, "James Cone and Recent Catholic Episcopal Teaching on Racism," 729.

73. Massingale, "James Cone and Recent Catholic Episcopal Teaching on Racism," 729.

Further Reading

- Laurie M. Cassidy and Alex Mikulich, eds., *Interrupting White Privilege: Catholic Theologians Break the Silence* (Maryknoll, NY: Orbis Books, 2007).
- M. Shawn Copeland, ed., *Uncommon Faithfulness: The Black Catholic Experience* (Maryknoll, NY: Orbis Books, 2009).
- M. Shawn Copeland, "White Supremacy and Anti-Black Logics in the Making of U.S. Catholicism," in *Anti-Blackness and Christian Ethics*, ed. Vincent W. Lloyd and Andrew Prevot (Maryknoll, NY: Orbis Books, 2017), 61–76.
- Matthew J. Cressler, *Authentically Black and Truly Catholic: The Rise of Black Catholicism in the Great Migration* (New York: New York University Press, 2017).
- Cyprian Davis, *The History of Black Catholics in the United States* (New York: Crossroad, 1990).
- Bryan N. Massingale, "James Cone and Recent Catholic Episcopal Teaching on Racism," *Theological Studies* 61 (2000): 700–730.
- Bryan N. Massingale, *Racial Justice and the Catholic Church* (Maryknoll, NY: Orbis Books, 2010).
- Alex Mikulich, Laurie Cassidy, and Margaret Pfeil, *The Scandal of White Complicity in US Hyper-Incarceration: A Nonviolent Spirituality of White Resistance* (New York: Palgrave Macmillan, 2013).
- Jon Nilson, *Hearing Past the Pain: Why White Catholic Theologians Need Black Theology* (New York: Paulist Press, 2007).
- Dawn M. Nothwehr, *That They May Be One: Catholic Social Teaching on Racism, Tribalism, and Xenophobia* (Maryknoll, NY: Orbis Books, 2008).

- Jamie T. Phelps, ed., *Black and Catholic: The Challenge and Gift of Black Folk* (Milwaukee: Marquette University Press, 2002).
- Andrew Prevot, *Theology and Race: Black and Womanist Traditions in the United States* (Leiden: Brill, 2018).
- Olga Segura, *Birth of a Movement: Black Lives Matter and the Catholic Church* (Maryknoll, NY: Orbis Books, 2021).
- Olga Segura, "I Reached Out to Every U.S. Diocese. Here Are the Ones Implementing the 2018 Pastoral Letter on Racism," *America*, November 21, 2019, https://www.americamagazine.org/faith/2019/11/21/i-reached-out-every-us-diocese-here-are-ones-implementing-2018-pastoral-letter.
- Karen Teel, *Racism and the Image of God* (New York: Palgrave Macmillan, 2010).

6

How to Be More of an Ally and Less of a Problem

It is my hope that if you have made it this far in the book, then you are at least interested in doing something more about the state of racial injustice in society and the Church. Like so many important areas of Christian concern for justice, peace, and the integrity of creation, the reality of racism and white supremacy can seem too overwhelming, too big an issue for any one person to address head-on. In response, some people—especially white people—understandably flustered by the magnitude of systemic injustices, throw their hands up and surrender to a state of indifference. Pope Francis has spoken about this temptation and tendency frequently over the years. In his 2013 apostolic exhortation *The Joy of the Gospel*, he acknowledged the overwhelming circumstances of evil and injustice in our world, warning with the example of economic inequality that "casual indifference in the face of such questions empties our lives and our words of all meaning."[1] Two years later, when confronting the crisis of global climate change in his encyclical letter *Laudato*

---

[1]. Francis, *Evangelii Gaudium*, 2013, no. 203, http://www.vatican.va/content/francesco/en/apost_exhortations/documents/papa-francesco_esortazione-ap_20131124_evangelii-gaudium.html.

Si', On Care for Our Common Home, he exhorted the faithful to recognize that we must not allow ourselves to shut down in the face of overwhelming suffering, but instead we should recall our inherent unity. "We need to strengthen the conviction that we are one single human family. There are no frontiers or barriers, political or social, behind which we can hide, still less is there room for the globalization of indifference."[2] At the end of *Laudato Si'*, Pope Francis explicitly prays that all the faithful "avoid the *sin* of indifference," naming in plain language that an authentic Christian response to seemingly overwhelming injustices in our world can never include merely shutting down and doing nothing.[3]

Like growing economic inequality and global climate change, racism and white supremacy appear to many well-meaning white people as overwhelming realities—systemic, structural, and institutional sins that an individual can hardly seem capable of adequately addressing. And yet, part of the Christian message is that God's love and grace can overcome even the most seemingly insurmountable obstacles, including death itself (see Romans 8:31–39). But here's the thing: Catholics do not believe in a "helicopter God" who merely appears from above to magically solve all the ills of human society and communal living. God has given each of us the gift of free will, which we have to exercise in cooperation with God's grace. One cannot simply will an end to racism or any other kind of systemic injustice in our world. We each consciously have to learn and reflect and act to make such changes. This requires great humility, patience, and vulnerability by all of us, particularly those of us who are white.

[2.] Francis, *Laudato Si', On Care for Our Common Home* (2015), no. 52 and *passim*, http://www.vatican.va/content/francesco/en/encyclicals/documents/papa-francesco_20150524_enciclica-laudato-si.html.

[3.] Francis, *Laudato Si'*, no. 246, emphasis added.

So far this book has presented an overview of the complex realities of racism and white supremacy in the United States, with the aim of providing white Catholics with a foundation for understanding something that, by virtue of our shared white racialized identities, we are dissuaded from recognizing and permitted to simply ignore by virtue of our privilege in an unjust society. We looked at what it means to understand and talk about racism; considered the meaning and consequences of whiteness; explored how systemic racism is irrefutably a white problem; examined the systemic, structural, and institutional nature of racism and white supremacy; and reflected on what the Catholic Church has said about racism in the United States and around the globe.

Now we shift gears in order to reflect on how white Catholics might be better allies in the quest with our BIPOC sisters and brothers to dismantle systemic racism and white supremacy in our communities and churches. It should go without saying that this chapter is not an exhaustive "how-to guide" for white people but an overview and introduction to some of the basic principles that we should be mindful of in order to be more of an ally and less of a problem. Given that I am also a white Catholic, susceptible to the same snares of being positioned by our society and Church in what Isabel Wilkerson aptly calls the "dominant caste," what follows in this chapter is as much a reminder and instruction for me as it is for you. Genuine advocacy requires openness to conversion and the humility to risk vulnerability and discomfort. In this chapter, I follow the lead of anti-racist scholars and activists, many of whom have studied, lived, and risked much for the sake of racial justice in our communities. As I continue to learn from them, especially my sisters and brothers of color, I invite you to learn as well and put into practice what you have learned.

Recognize the Significance of Your Social Location

Almost a decade ago I stood outside a sushi restaurant in a Boston neighborhood near the university where I had been working on my graduate studies. I was there to meet a friend of mine, also a graduate student, though he was younger than me and was a few years behind me in the doctoral program. I was excited to catch up with him over some good food and looked forward to our conversation. When he arrived, we went in and were seated at a table, ordered our food, and began a lively conversation that ranged from departmental gossip to esoteric theological and philosophical topics. I was having a great time and enjoying our food, conversation, and company, and I thought that my friend was too, until he stopped talking. It took me a minute to realize something was wrong. So I asked if everything was okay, to which he responded that I kept interrupting him and talking over him as he tried to speak. I was shocked. I was confused. I immediately began reviewing in my head what had transpired in our conversation so far. Did I say something wrong? Had I been talking over him? Could I have been unwittingly interrupting him without an ounce of awareness?

I'm ashamed to say that my initial reaction was not productive. My biased answers to my own internal inquiry produced an "all clear" result, which led me to become defensive in the face of the accusation that I was somehow doing something rude or inconsiderate or mean. I certainly did not feel I like I was doing that, let alone ever having *intended* to do so. Up to that point, I was having a genuinely good time and was intellectually engaged in this conversation with my friend. When I get excited and enthusiastic about subjects that I care about deeply, I know I can get animated. I tried to explain that to my friend. I shared how I love to discuss and debate the kinds of things we were talking about, and how much I was enjoying our conversation and how appreciative I was of his insights and contributions. I recall saying that there must have been a misunderstanding, a mistake that led to a misreading of my behavior or intentions. I unthinkingly began to assume *he had made an error* and tacitly started *blaming him*.

There was indeed a misunderstanding and a mistake, but it was not on my friend's side of the table. It was all mine.

My friend, who is a Black man, tried at the time to explain to me that he had lived his whole adult life with white people interrupting him, speaking over him, dismissing him, disregarding him, and worse. What was transpiring between us, even as friends and academic colleagues at an enjoyable dinner out, was triggering for him because, given his lifelong experience of navigating through a systemically racist and white supremacist society, I was unthinkingly exercising a form of white dominance and privilege. He was entirely right, but I did not understand it at the time. So I responded as most well-meaning white people typically respond when called out on their subtly racist behaviors (sometimes called microaggressions)—I felt hurt and got defensive.

In hindsight, I can recognize the unreflective behaviors, presuppositions, and attitudes that I was socialized to exhibit in my day-to-day life that led to that exchange. So subtle are some of these behaviors that they can be very difficult at times to recognize, especially if you, like me, are a beneficiary of a racist system that shields you from seeing actions that you might not ever consider transgressive or rude as nevertheless demeaning and harmful to people of color. Because much of my previous experience of such animated and engaged conversations had taken place almost exclusively with white interlocutors, I (wrongly) perceived my behavior as normal, appropriate, and unassailable (hence my initial defensiveness). Being called out for a behavior that seemed like second nature felt like an attack on my personhood or personality rather than what it actually was: an act of kindness and trust, as well as an invitation to reevaluate my unconscious behavior. At the time, I couldn't understand what was different about the way I interacted with my Black friend and the way I interacted with my white friends. Now, however, I recognize that I had not taken into consideration the significance of my social location and the consequences of unexamined white performance for those around me. Good intentions are not sufficient for preventing racist behaviors, especially when we step back and think about how deeply ingrained such patterns of thinking and acting are for whites in our world and Church.

In a white supremacist society such as the United States, where the white population is given all sorts of unearned advantages, there is bestowed on those considered "white" a kind of power, as we examined in chapters 2 and 3. This is the heart of "white privilege," that much of what white people like me consider to be innocent behaviors, thoughts, and attitudes is in fact shaped and informed by racist socialization. The consequences of this are not readily apparent to most white people, at least not at first or not without significant work and learning. One of the first things that is required of white Catholics who wish to be anti-racist allies is to become aware of (a) your distinctive social location and (b) the manifold significance of the social location you occupy, including the intended and unintended consequences of your particular socialization. This is more challenging than it might seem. For example, not all white people occupy the exact same social location. There are multiple kinds of social oppression and advantage, such as those related to gender, sexual orientation, citizenship status, class, and ability. And in the Church, you can add clerical status in contrast to the laity, as a consequence of the deeply ingrained injustice of clericalism. Learning to see where one stands in an unjust social system means recognizing the intersectionality of all our identities.[4] The various and simultaneous ways we understand ourselves or are classified by the society in which we live compound our identities and affect how each of us sees, understands, behaves in, and experiences the world.

In the case of that dinner years ago with my friend, I had not considered any of the things about my social location—being a white male or a Catholic priest, for example—that conferred on me layers of unacknowledged power, privilege, and protection. Operating from that social location shielded me—not just at that particular dinner but also nearly always—from having to consider how my actions or words may have unintentionally harmed others. Our unjust racist and white supremacist society conferred on me power that I didn't realize I had—power that, left unacknowledged and unredeemed, would continue to be deployed to harm others, even when I did not intend it, even when I thought of myself as an anti-racist ally.

As the anti-racist activist and author Layla Saad keenly states, "The first thing to understand is that allyship is not an identity but a practice."[5] In order for white people like us to be more of an ally and less of a problem, we need to interrogate our preconceptions and examine our actions and habits. Learning

---

[4]. For more on intersectionality, see Patricia Hill Collins and Sirma Bilge, *Intersectionality* (Cambridge, UK: Polity Press, 2016).

[5]. Layla F. Saad, *Me and White Supremacy: Combat Racism, Change the World, and Become a Good Ancestor* (Naperville, IL: Sourcebooks, 2020), 125–26. This is also something that the Jewish anti-racist writer Paul Kivel stated in *Uprooting Racism: How White People Can Work for Racial Justice*, 3rd ed. (Vancouver: New Society, 2011), 116.

to recognize that the way you see and experience the world as a white person is at times very different from the way BIPOC see and experience the world is something that requires humility and a willingness to be vulnerable and nondefensive when confronted about your problematic assumptions or behaviors. Explaining within the context of white fragility, Saad unpacks what is required for white people to begin the journey toward allyship.

> White fragility thus makes you an unreliable ally to BIPOC, because you do not have the resiliency needed to talk about racism. When your BIPOC coworker, friend, or family member shares with you an experience of racism they have been through, you are unable to hear them. You try to convince them they are imagining it or are reading too much into the situation. That they have misunderstood what was said or done—that it was not about race but about something else. Rather than allowing yourself to really hear what they are going through and ask with empathy and compassion how you can support them, you minimize their experiences and let them know, without saying it, that you are not a safe white person for them to be around. As much as you think you have convinced yourself and them with these explanations, all you have done is make clear your level of white fragility around racial conversations.[6]

Saad describes well exactly the dynamics that were at play during that dinner with my friend in Boston. It was my white fragility—my inability in the moment to truly listen, to set aside my presumptions, to be a real friend—that was on display in my shame, confusion, and defensiveness.

---

[6]. Saad, *Me and White Supremacy*, 44.

That dinner episode is important, not because it was a singular or rare event in my personal history but rather because I was able after the fact to see what really happened and try to learn from it. And it has stayed with me. I am sure that there are many other times I have unwittingly harmed or retraumatized a friend, coworker, or stranger because of my own ignorance and lack of recognition of racist and white supremacist dynamics at work. But too often my white privilege prevents me from easily seeing them. Only in learning to be deliberately attentive to these dynamics and how they operate every day in your life can you begin to change them and therefore begin striving to be more of an ally and less of a problem.

Relearn What You Thought You Knew

By virtue of being white in a systemically racist and white supremacist society, we have been socialized and led to believe that the world revolves around us—or, if not you and me specifically, then at least the people collectively categorized as "white." We saw this in chapter 2 when we explored the pervasiveness of white normativity in American culture, and we have that sense of white hegemony constantly reinscribed in us by popular culture, media, and society, as we saw in chapter 3. All of the big and little, overt and tacit ways that we have been fed the lie of racism's normalcy and the "objectivity" of white supremacy have to be dismantled if we hope to have any chance of being a true ally in the quest for racial justice. Summarizing well the context into which many of us white folks were born, raised, and currently live, Saad explains:

> White supremacy is a system you have been born into. Whether or not you have known it, it is a system that has granted you unearned privileges, protection, and

power. It is also a system that has been designed to keep you asleep and unaware of what having that privilege, protection, and power has meant for people who do not look like you. What you receive for your whiteness comes at a steep cost for those who are not white. This may sicken you and cause you to feel guilt, anger, and frustration. But you cannot change your white skin color to stop receiving these privileges, just like BIPOC cannot change their skin color to stop receiving racism. But what you *can* do is wake up to what is really going on.[7]

This brings us to another element of what it means to strive to be a genuine ally—namely, "waking up," as Saad put it, to the world as it actually is and not as we white people have been led to believe it is.

To "wake up to what is really going on" requires openness to relearning a lot of what you previously assumed to be the case about yourself, others, society, and the Church. In order really to be receptive to a paradigm shift in our thinking, we have to be willing to seek answers and information from sources that we may previously have ignored or about which we have been unaware. Robin DiAngelo explains: "We can get it in several interconnected ways. We can seek out the information from books, websites, films, and other available sources. Many people of color *are* committed to teaching whites about racism (on their own terms) and have been offering this information to us for decades, if not centuries."[8] It isn't that learning about the reality and extent of racial injustice and white privilege requires a

---

[7]. Saad, *Me and White Supremacy*, 14.

[8]. Robin DiAngelo, *White Fragility: Why It's So Hard for White People to Talk about Racism* (Boston: Beacon Books, 2018), 146.

gnostic quest for some kind of hidden, secret knowledge. It's just that we need the humility to recognize that the unjust systems in which we have been socialized work to prevent white people from seeing the full picture. Therefore, we have to work at it. On this point, DiAngelo adds: "It is our own lack of interest or motivation that has prevented us from receiving it."[9]

One of the primary reasons that white people in the United States have not engaged the complex and challenging history of racial injustice in this country is that most of us are afraid of being uncomfortable. Truth be told, it's not really a conscious fear of discomfort but a consistent conflation of "being uncomfortable" with "being threatened." As Bryan Massingale states clearly, "There is no way to tell the truth about race in this country without white people becoming uncomfortable. Because the plain truth is that if it were up to people of color, racism would have been resolved, over and done, a long time ago. *The only reason for racism's persistence is that white people continue to benefit from it.*"[10] It does not get much clearer than that. If you want to be a white ally in the cause of racial justice, then you have to be willing to risk discomfort and vulnerability. As Massingale adds, "Avoiding and sugarcoating this truth is killing people of color. Silence for the sake of making white people comfortable is a luxury we can no longer afford." He advises would-be white allies further: "Stay in the discomfort, the anxiety, the guilt, the shame, the anger. Because only when a critical mass of white folks are outraged, grieved, and pained over the status quo—only when white people become upset

---

[9]. DiAngelo, *White Fragility*, 146.

[10]. Bryan N. Massingale, "The Assumptions of White Privilege and What We Can Do about It," *National Catholic Reporter*, June 1, 2020, emphasis original, https://www.ncronline.org/news/opinion/assumptions-white-privilege-and-what-we-can-do-about-it.

enough to declare, 'This cannot and will not be!'—only then will real change begin to become a possibility."[11]

Motivated by our faith and our conviction that racial injustice and white supremacy are not only intolerable but also evils that should be completely eradicated, we must risk the vulnerability and stand in the discomfort that serious learning and discussions about race entail. What is also required is, as Massingale puts it, the need for white people to "admit [our] ignorance and do something about it."[12] The only way to *relearn* what we thought we knew is first to *unlearn* the falsehoods white people have been taught in order actually to *learn* the truth. And nobody else can do that for us. It is the responsibility and moral duty of each of us to educate ourselves to be better anti-racist allies. Far too often, well-meaning white people who are moved by the stark examples of racial injustice in their communities move quickly to put Black people and other people of color on the spot, requesting—sometimes *demanding*—that they "educate us" about what we, as white people, had previously overlooked or misunderstood. That is not the appropriate answer. Despite what might feel like a genuine desire to learn and change, such behavior is reflective of white privilege in action—acting as if people of color are merely means to your educational- and personal-growth ends. This kind of solicitation not only runs the very real risk of instrumentalizing people of color for white benefit but it also risks tokenism and retraumatizing victims of racial oppression. It is *not* the job of BIPOC to "educate" white people about the horrendous truths of racism, white supremacy, and the national history we have collectively sanitized for white comfort. That information is out

---

11. Massingale, "The Assumptions of White Privilege and What We Can Do about It."

12. Massingale, "The Assumptions of White Privilege and What We Can Do about It."

there; resources are abundant (including the dozens of books recommended in this book for further reading). As DiAngelo notes, "To break with the conditioning of whiteness—the conditioning that makes us apathetic about racism and prevents us from developing the skills we need to interrupt it—white people need to find out for themselves what they can do. There is so much excellent advice out there today—written by both people of color and white people."[13]

It is important to recall that educating oneself is both a beginning and a lifelong process for white people. It is a beginning in the sense that reading some books, watching some films, attending some lectures, or engaging in meaningful conversations about race and racism do not constitute a one-time corrective or all-encompassing panacea. Just like all forms of human knowledge, the learning we must do as white Catholics is something that is ongoing. On this point, it is also a lifelong process for white people because we still live in a world and in a context that is conditioned by anti-Black racism and white supremacy. As such, there are always systems, structures, and institutions working in subtle and complex ways to cover over the truths we white people learn when we listen to, reflect on, incorporate, and constructively respond to our sisters and brothers of color. This is why it is so important for white people to do their homework first, including the self-reflection and examination of conscience necessary to come to conversations about race with a nondefensive posture and a willingness to rest in a place of discomfort in order to learn and grow. One book or a dozen books will never be enough, but they will be a start and a positive sign of your sincerity in trying to be a good anti-racist ally.

---

[13]. DiAngelo, *White Fragility*, 144.

In Lin-Manuel Miranda's highly acclaimed musical *Hamilton*, there is a line sung by the sometimes-narrator and eventual-antagonist Aaron Burr to the show's protagonist, Alexander Hamilton. It is a small bit of advice given to an enthusiastic young politician and aspiring public figure. His recommendation is for Hamilton to "talk less, smile more." I think about that line often when talking with fellow white people who want to know what they can do once they begin, as Saad put it, to "wake up" to the reality of racism. White people in America are socialized to think they are smarter, better, more skilled, entitled, and should always be in charge. It is this presumption that leads to awkward and sometimes violent confrontations in retail stores when entitled white patrons demand to "speak to the manager" of a given establishment, only to discover that they were already speaking to the person in charge, who happened to be a person of color. It is this presumption that leads to underqualified white people being promoted over and given more opportunities than people of color in all sorts of sectors of society. It is this presumption that led the Trappist monk and best-selling author Thomas Merton to critique those he called "white liberals" of the 1960s civil rights era because these ostensibly sympathetic northern whites—many of whom were religious leaders, including Catholic priests and sisters—were quick to insert themselves into the cause for racial justice as long as they were ultimately calling the shots and receiving the credit.[14]

An essential aspect of being a genuine white ally in the work for racial justice is *listening*—real, sincere, active *listening*. And the only way that happens is for white people to be quiet for a change. In describing ways that a white ally can contribute to

---

14. See Thomas Merton, "Letters to a White Liberal," in *Seeds of Destruction* (New York: Farrar, Straus and Giroux, 1964), 3–71.

the cause of racial justice, the anti-racist writer Paul Kivel notes: "This includes listening to people of color so that we can support the actions they take, the risks they bear in defending their lives and challenging white hegemony. It includes analyzing the struggle of white people to maintain dominance and the struggle of people of color to gain equal opportunity and justice."[15] To be an ally is to be an authentic supporter whose actions align with the righteous mission for racial justice in order to bring about a different kind of world, one that is built on justice and peace rather than prejudice and discrimination. Massingale observes that to "create a different world, we must learn how this one came to be. And unlearn what we previously took for granted. This means that we have to read. And learn from perspectives of people of color."[16]

Kivel lists a number of recommendations for those white people who wish to be allies. These include recognizing that racism is always and everywhere present and operative; attuning oneself to notice "who is the center of attention and who is the center of power" in various sectors of our communities; noticing "how racism is denied, minimized, and justified" by other white people; learning to see the intersectional connections between racial oppression and other forms of violence, marginalization, and oppression; prioritizing "support for leadership of people of color," especially in racial-justice movements; and talking "with your children and other young people about racism."[17] This last point is an important one and something that other anti-racist scholars and activists, particularly those of color, talk about consistently.

---

[15]. Kivel, *Uprooting Racism*, 116–17.

[16]. Massingale, "The Assumptions of White Privilege and What We Can Do about It."

[17]. Kivel, *Uprooting Racism*, 120–21.

It is not enough merely to educate yourself, listen to others, and then determine that your work is done because your personal views and outlook have changed. One of the most difficult responsibilities for white allies is what Massingale calls having "the courage to confront your family and friends."[18] What he is describing is the "pass" that many white people give one another when faced with a statement, expression, perspective, or behavior that we recognize as inherently racist or white supremacist. We "let it go" because the person is a family member, friend, neighbor, coworker, classmate, and so on. We convince ourselves that it's "not worth the trouble" to speak up, or we fear offending the other person or embarrassing them. The classic example of this is the cultural cliché of the old aunt, uncle, or grandparent at the Thanksgiving dinner table. Many of us white people witness small and large racist behaviors, often when the group is exclusively or predominantly white, and we rationalize our refusal to speak up on account of the person's age or our presumption of their intention or something else. But we cannot be genuine allies if we only strive to be anti-racists when it is easy or comfortable. That kind of approach amounts to withdrawing into the safety and security of white privilege, where we white folks have the luxury of choosing to confront the evils of racism and white supremacy or not as we feel like it. As Kivel reminds us, "People of color will always be on the front lines fighting racism because their lives are at stake."[19] And as Massingale notes, "Until white people call out white people, there will always be safe places for racial ugliness to brew and fester."[20]

---

[18]. Massingale, "The Assumptions of White Privilege and What We Can Do about It."

[19]. Kivel, *Uprooting Racism*, 117.

[20]. Massingale, "The Assumptions of White Privilege and What We Can Do about It."

The work of educating ourselves and learning from others—especially people of color—is not for our own self-gratification or interest but to aid in the transformation of an unjust society toward one of justice and peace. That requires of us the courage to stand up and help our fellow whites see what we have come to see and help them join us in the work that we are committing ourselves to pursue in order that we might all live in a better world. As the artist Courtney Ariel wrote in an essay directed at potential white allies, "I believe that this is holy work, the work of justice, the pursuit of it. It doesn't need an audience, and it will not always have one."[21] Not only is this holy work but it is also absolutely essential work. The sad and painful truth is that Black lives and the lives of other people of color are at stake. To avoid doing the right thing for the sake of our personal comfort is an affront to the inherent dignity and value of our sisters and brothers of color whose lives and safety hang in the balance on account of systemic racism and white supremacy.

Develop a Spirituality of Ongoing Conversion

Despite the popular conception of conversion as an immediate, all-at-once experience, the Christian understanding of conversion—from the Latin *conversio,* "to turn around"—is actually a lifelong process. Rather than the common Latinate word "conversion," it might be better for us to draw from the ancient Christian usage of the Greek word *metanoia,* which means "transformation," particularly of one's heart and mind. The concept of *metanoia* reflects the Christian view that

---

[21]. Courtney Ariel, "For Our White Friends Desiring to Be Allies," *Sojourners,* August 16, 2017, https://sojo.net/articles/our-white-friends-desiring-be-allies.

discipleship is not a one-time thing but a lifelong journey toward transformation from selfishness to generosity, from hate to love, from division to healing. This is the message that Jesus proclaims in the gospels when he calls his followers—all of whom, like us, are flawed and imperfect—and invites them to see the world differently and live in a new way. This new way of being is, as St. Paul described it, a rejection of what is presented as the "wisdom" or status quo of the world in order to embrace the wisdom of God, which appears like "foolishness" to those who live and operate according to the ways of an unjust society (see 1 Cor 1:18–31).

This clarification about how we understand the ongoing journey of Christian conversion (*metanoia*) is important for the work of racial justice because neither is accomplished overnight or in short order. God gives us the grace to respond to the invitation, but it is up to us to commit and recommit ourselves to the challenging work of living as better followers of Christ. This work entails, for us white Catholics especially, striving to be better allies in the work for racial justice. As Massingale has made clear, for Catholics racial justice is a pro-life issue. Massingale notes that this is also something John Paul II stated loud and clear during his final visit to the United States in 1999, when he admonished Catholics to "eradicate every form of racism" as part of their avowed commitment to life issues.[22] This truth is not always readily received by many fellow Christians, some of whom have been coopted by American political talking points that seek to diminish the urgency and importance of anti-racist activism. Gloria Purvis, a Black Catholic journalist, made this point publicly during the summer of 2020, which led

---

22. Massingale, "The Assumptions of White Privilege and What We Can Do about It."

to a significant amount of pushback from many conservative Catholics.[23] And yet, to be an authentic Catholic is to be, as Massingale says, "unconditionally pro-life,"[24] which is not about simply picking and choosing which life issues one finds most comfortable or appealing but is instead about embracing the truth of every person's inherent dignity and value. This is not, by any means, an easy task. As we have seen so far in this book, it requires a lot of learning, thinking, and praying—all of which must be done in a spirit of openness and humility.

There is a saying that is very common in ministry circles and among other helping professions that "you cannot give what you do not have." The basic idea here is that the work of justice is *hard* work, and seeking to live the Christian life with authenticity is *challenging*. There is nothing easy about confronting structures of injustice that literally take the lives of women, men, and children on a daily basis. The ways of thinking and being in the world that make racism and white supremacy normative in our society are deeply ingrained; many people, many *white people*, are invested in maintaining the status quo, even if they are not always conscious of what is really happening. For people of faith, to stand up to such hatred, division, sin, and evil requires being

---

[23.] See Heidi Schlumpf, "Paying the Price for Anti-Racism Work," *National Catholic Reporter*, July 1, 2020, https://www.ncronline.org/news/opinion/ncr-connections/paying-price-anti-racism-work; Samuel D. Rocha, "An Interview with EWTN's Gloria Purvis," *Church Life Journal*, July 20, 2020, https://churchlifejournal.nd.edu/articles/the-gift-of-blackness/; and Elizabeth Bruenig, "'Racism Makes a Liar of God': How the American Catholic Church Is Wrestling with the Black Lives Matter Movement," *New York Times*, August 6, 2020, https://www.nytimes.com/2020/08/06/opinion/sunday/gloria-purvis-george-floyd-blm.html.

[24.] Massingale, "The Assumptions of White Privilege and What We Can Do about It."

well grounded, spiritually nourished, and imbued with the living Word of God. The Black feminist scholar, activist, and poet Audre Lorde once wrote, "Caring for myself is not self-indulgence, it is self-preservation, and that is an act of political warfare."[25] This is an important motto for white Catholics committed to being better allies to recall. You cannot run on empty, because you cannot effect consequential change or have a lasting positive impact without grounding yourself in your faith and caring for yourself physically, mentally, emotionally, and spiritually. Such care is, as Lorde reminds us, not "self-indulgent" but absolutely necessary to maintain the integrity of our faith, motives, and perspective. However, it is also important for white Catholics to discern between "self-care" and "white comfort." The former is essential, while the latter can become a justification for our own resistance, inaction, or dismissal of the many difficult and unsettling truths about the reality of racism and privilege that white people like us are already inclined to avoid.

Further highlighting the importance of grounding one's commitment to working for racial justice in one's faith and spirituality, Massingale acknowledges that racism is indeed "a political issue and a social divide," but also, "at its deepest level, racism is a soul sickness." With a particularly Catholic approach, Massingale explains the importance of prayer in anti-racist work.

> This soul sickness can only be healed by deep prayer. Yes, we need social reforms. We need equal educational opportunities, changed police practices, equitable access to health care, an end to employment and housing discrimination. But only an invasion of divine love

---

[25.] See Audre Lorde, *A Burst of Light and Other Essays* (New York: Dover Books, 2017), 130.

will shatter the small images of God that enable us to live undisturbed by the racism that benefits some and terrorizes so many.[26]

For white Catholics committed to being better Christian disciples and allies to our Black sisters and brothers, as well as to other people of color, prayer is absolutely essential.

It is my hope that this book offers fellow white Catholics a helpful set of resources to aid in developing a spirituality of ongoing conversion, one centered on Christ's message of justice and peace, which requires a strong grounding in a life of prayer. It is important to remember that we never do the work of God alone, but always as part of and within the broader community of the faithful. We are united to one another through baptism and in the Holy Spirit. As Catholic Christians, we can work with folks of other faiths or no faith tradition at all in the spirit of human solidarity, but we know that our personal strength to be vulnerable, our courage to learn and relearn uncomfortable truths, and our openness to work for racial justice are made possible by our faith tradition and baptismal vocations.

Further Reading

- Courtney Ariel, "For Our White Friends Desiring to Be Allies," *Sojourners,* August 16, 2017, https://sojo.net/articles/our-white-friends-desiring-be-allies.
- JLove Calderon and Tim Wise, "Code of Ethics for White Anti-Racists," Medium, June 16, 2020, https://medium.com/@timjwise/code-of-ethics-for-white-anti-racists-103914639dd7.

[26.] Massingale, "The Assumptions of White Privilege and What We Can Do about It."

- Michael Eric Dyson, *Tears We Cannot Stop: A Sermon to White America* (New York: St. Martin's Press, 2017).
- Jeannine Hill Fletcher, *The Sin of White Supremacy: Christianity, Racism, and Religious Diversity in America* (Maryknoll, NY: Orbis Books, 2017).
- Paul Kivel, *Uprooting Racism: How White People Can Work for Racial Justice*, 3rd ed. (Vancouver: New Society, 2011).
- Bryan N. Massingale, "The Assumptions of White Privilege and What We Can Do about It," *National Catholic Reporter*, June 1, 2020, https://www.ncronline.org/news/opinion/assumptions-white-privilege-and-what-we-can-do-about-it.
- Bryan N. Massingale, *Racial Justice and the Catholic Church* (Maryknoll, NY: Orbis Books, 2010).
- Ijeoma Oluo, *So You Want to Talk about Race* (New York: Seal Press, 2019).
- Layla F. Saad, *Me and White Supremacy: Combat Racism, Change the World, and Become a Good Ancestor* (Naperville, IL: Sourcebooks, 2020).
- George Yancy, ed., *White Self-Criticality beyond Anti-Racism: How Does It Feel to Be a White Problem?* (Lanham, MD: Lexington Books, 2015).

7

Where Do We Go from Here?

> Now, this is not called morality, this is not called faith, this has nothing to do with Christ. It has to do with power, and part of the dilemma of the Christian Church is the fact that it opted, in fact, for power and betrayed its own first principles which were a responsibility to every living soul, the assumption of which the Christian Church's basis, as I understand it, is that *all* men are the sons of God and that *all* men are free in the eyes of God and are victims of the commandment given to the Christian Church, "Love one another as I have loved you."
>
> —James Baldwin,
> "White Racism or World Community?"[1]

The most fundamental principle of Catholic moral theology is the inherent dignity and value of the human person. That God loves each person into existence, that each person is created in the image and likeness of God, grounds all the central themes of

---

[1]. James Baldwin, "White Racism or World Community?," in *James Baldwin: Collected Essays*, ed. Toni Morrison (New York: Library of America, 1998), 752.

how we are called to live with one another in community. It is this principle that motivates the Church's view that every life is sacred, regardless of which stage in life a person may find oneself in or what attributes are associated with the individual. When people of various faiths, or no faith tradition at all, cry out in collective lamentation the words "Black Lives Matter," it should invoke for Christians this basic moral claim to the universal dignity, value, import, and sacredness of human life. It should, as it is intended rhetorically, call to mind the fact that too many people—Christians included—have failed to embrace this moral principle and have not adequately embodied its truth. It should challenge us white Christians in particular to reexamine not only our own ways of thinking and acting in the world but also why our systems, structures, and institutions continue to operate in such a way as to necessitate protests and placards and chants to draw attention to the fact that not all lives are, in practice, treated as mattering, meaningful, dignified, or valued, even if in theory we Christians claim this to be divinely revealed.

The quote from James Baldwin that opens this chapter speaks to precisely this point. As we have seen throughout this book, no aspect of our social or ecclesial contexts can escape the racist history and culture of the United States. Sadly, this also includes the Catholic Church. Baldwin adroitly diagnoses the uncomfortable problem with American Christianity—namely, that the Church has too often chosen "power" over "its own first principles," such as the universal dignity and value of all human life. And power in the American context is always tied in some way to race, which means in this case that power is tied to whiteness. We have seen how white normativity has both shaped the Church and shielded its majority-white leadership and membership from fully recognizing the depth and breadth of racial injustice and white privilege in the Church and broader society.

Much of this book has been focused on educating white Catholics about the complexities and nuances of systemic racism and white privilege. The intention was invitational. I wished to respectfully and lovingly challenge my white sisters and brothers to see reality as it actually is in society and the Church, rather than hold on to the myths and falsities white people too often unwittingly or deliberately embrace. This is not an easy task, nor is it a short-term process. I know from my own experience that a spirituality of ongoing conversion is necessary because we white folks are generally formed and live in contexts that shield us from the truth of racial injustice and reinforce false narratives supporting a worldview that can only accurately be described in terms of white supremacy. I believe that the first steps toward substantive change and correction are for white people to do their homework; educate themselves; learn from the range of resources out there, especially by people of color; and engage in self-reflection and an examination of conscience in order to be in a position ready for allyship and support. Shortly before his assassination in 1968, Martin Luther King Jr. wrote about the need for white people to educate themselves and others, noting that the structures of white supremacy discourage us white folks from seeing and accepting our own racial ignorance. "Whites, it must frankly be said, are not putting in a similar mass effort to reeducate themselves out of their racial ignorance. It is an aspect of their sense of superiority that the white people of America believe they have so little to learn."[2]

But it is not enough to go it alone or merely to stop at the transformation of your own individual outlook and understanding—as important as that is. Because racism is systemic and

---

2. Martin Luther King Jr., *Where Do We Go from Here: Chaos or Community?* (Boston: Beacon Books, 1968), 10.

cultural, there are bigger forces at work that need addressing and, as we saw in chapter 4, there are systems, structures, and institutions that must be changed. While change begins within each person, the spirit of ongoing conversion we are invited to cultivate should subsequently lead us outside ourselves to work with others on a collective level. In the previous chapter we looked at how each of us can work to become more of an ally and less of a problem. In this concluding chapter, I want to invite us to consider some ways we white people can work together with our sisters and brothers of color to advocate for change regarding racial justice. I have organized some starting points and suggestions for anti-racist advocacy and action at the personal, local, and national levels. This is by no means an exhaustive list. Rather, it is intended to be a brief introduction to a broader range of collective possibilities in our effort to promote and support racial justice in our communities.

At the Personal and Family Level

There is an instructive passage in the gospels about Jesus' ministry and how those who knew him best received his preaching and deeds. Matthew's account tells us that Jesus returned to his hometown and "began to teach the people in their synagogue, so that they were astounded and said, 'Where did this man get this wisdom and these deeds of power? Is not this the carpenter's son? Is not his mother called Mary?'" (Mt 13:54–55). While those who witnessed Jesus grow up from a child into a young man and saw that he had now become an influential preacher and prophetic figure were at first astounded, they quickly turned on him. Matthew's gospel tells us that they became offended by his words and actions. Jesus' response to their hostility and their resistance to his proclamation of the coming reign of God is an adage that speaks directly to the challenge of living and preaching the hard truths of faith among those to whom we are closest: "But Jesus said to them, 'Prophets are not without honor except in their own country and in their own house'" (Mt 13:57).

On some level we all know exactly what Jesus experienced and is talking about in this gospel passage. The positive side of the familiarity that comes with close family members, friends, and coworkers is that those relationships help to keep us grounded and support us when we are struggling. But the shadow side of such familiarity often surfaces when we must confront our family members, friends, or coworkers about something difficult, unsettling, or even dangerous. If we find ourselves in the uncomfortable but necessary situation of offering a loving yet challenging message to those we care about, there is always the risk that they will become defensive and dredge up in retaliation those things about us that we might prefer were left unsaid. In the context of a formal intervention about a loved one's substance abuse, the person being challenged might respond in kind with a question like: "Where did you get *this* wisdom? Aren't you the one who used to party hard in college?" Or in confronting a loved one about work habits and choices about time, they might respond with something like: "Where did you get *this* wisdom? Aren't you the one who has failed to hold down a steady job?" Deflection, justification, anger, and defensiveness are all real likelihoods when difficult subjects are broached and ways of thinking or behaviors are challenged, even when done with the best of intentions and in a patient and loving manner.

In chapter 1, I talked about how there are few things more incendiary than to call someone a racist. Given that most white people operate with an overly simplistic "commonsense" notion of racism, which says racists are bad people, it is not surprising that any conversation that hints at attitudes, behaviors, or outlooks as being racist might spark strong defensiveness. This is true with strangers, and it is also true with those close to us. The difference between these conversation partners is a matter of what is at stake. While the potential that some stranger will get angry and defensive with us in a conversation about racism or white privilege is always present, our personal investment in that individual is minimal. Fear of possibly upsetting a loved one or coworker with whom we might live or must continue to work, however, oftentimes preempts any action on our part. We just don't want to risk offending, hurting, or even losing this person in our lives. And so we say nothing.

White silence is itself a form of complicity. The temptation to silence is never stronger for white people than it is when we are around those we have known our entire lives, those we love and respect, those who may have raised us or have been raised alongside us. So commonplace is the setting for white silence that it has become a cliché to talk about the American Thanksgiving dinner table. After several hours of eating rich food and imbibing holiday drinks, the social inhibitions tend to be lifted and some family members—usually the older matriarchs or patriarchs or in-laws—tell an offensive joke or express a controversial political view or repeat a racist stereotype. In another setting, at another time, we might be inclined to speak up and at least register our displeasure with such a remark, perhaps offering a corrective or clarification in an attempt to help educate this person. But as the social cliché goes, uncomfortable family members lock eyes and shake heads and make excuses—"There goes Grandma again!" or "That's typical Uncle Bob!" But nobody confronts the giant elephant of racism in the room. Nobody among the majority or entirely white group at the table wants to rock the boat or risk a heated emotional blowup. We white people are inclined to justify a pass in this or that case, and for this or that person. We may convince ourselves—and sometimes even others—that we "cannot teach old dogs new tricks," justifying our silence on account of the improbability that the white person at the table will ever change.

While it may not seem to be the biggest issue or the greatest contribution to racism, our white silence in the face of everyday iterations of racist thinking and behaviors perpetuates a culture of racial injustice. It adds up over time. For most white people, talking about race in general, and racism in particular, can be an uneasy and even frightening prospect. But this is where our work must begin. The Second Vatican Council taught us that the "family is, so to speak, the domestic church."[3] Our families are where we first learn about God and share our faith with one another. Therefore, as people of faith, Catholics are called to address pressing issues of justice and peace within the context of our families. Furthermore, as John Paul II taught in his 1981 exhortation *Familiaris Consortio*, "The fostering of authentic and mature communion between persons within the family is the first and irreplaceable school of social life, and example and stimulus for the broader community relationships marked by respect, justice, dialogue, and love."[4] In other words, the family is the starting point and model for how we are to act in the broader Church and world. If we avoid important or sensitive issues within the family, how much more may we be inclined

---

[3.] Second Vatican Council, *Lumen Gentium*, 1964, no. 11, https://www.vatican.va/archive/hist_councils/ii_vatican_council/documents/vat-ii_const_19641121_lumen-gentium_en.html.

[4.] John Paul II, *Familiaris Consortio*, 1981, no. 43, http://www.vatican.va/content/john-paul-ii/en/apost_exhortations/documents/hf_jp-ii_exh_19811122_familiaris-consortio.html.

to avoid or dismiss them outside of it? The issues of racism and white privilege may appear daunting, and fear of rejection or anger may tempt us to avoid talking about these important topics, but to follow the example of Jesus in the gospels, we must not shy away from doing God's will even when it is tough.

This can take a number of forms. One simple way to begin facing the tough questions may be to assess our home environments for explicit or tacit evidence of systemic racism. We might ask ourselves what books, images, artwork, films, or other aspects of our shared environment reflect or suggest how we see the world, others, and ourselves. Anti-racism activist Paul Kivel writes that it is "even more important to discuss racism and to pay attention to our home if we have children." He adds: "As responsible parents, we need to think about the toys, games, computer games, dolls, books and pictures that our young ones are exposed to. It is not just children of color who need Latino/a, Asian American, Native American, and African American dolls. It is not just children of color who are hurt by computer games that portray people of color as evil, dangerous and expendable."[5] How "normalcy" is represented in what we present to children will affect how they view themselves and others. Serious reflection on whom and what cultures are represented in art, entertainment, and other media, including toys and video games, can help white people begin to take decisive action and make deliberate choices at home.

Language is also a very important element in anti-racism work, though it is often overlooked. What we say and how we say it reflects beliefs and assumptions that form our foundational worldviews. Systemic racism and the white privilege that is

---

5. Paul Kivel, *Uprooting Racism: How White People Can Work for Racial Justice*, 3rd ed. (Vancouver: New Society, 2011), 304.

tied to it are perpetuated through subtle signals that can be challenging for white people to recognize. Greater focus on what images we use, terms we employ, and assumptions about groups of people we express in our everyday conversations is also an important small step in our personal experience of ongoing conversion; it also can have significant impact on forming the next generation to be less racist. It is important to remember that racism is learned and privilege assumed. Therefore, we can change the curriculum of life that reinforces destructive patterns of thought, speech, and behavior. There is no more important place to do this than at home with those with whom we share our life and love.

At the Local Level

The anti-racism activist and author Ijeoma Oluo notes that many white people simply feel overwhelmed by the immensity of systemic racism and the injustices tied to white privilege. "It is easy to think that the problem of racial oppression in this country is just too big."[6] As a result, many people, including well-intentioned white people, simply conclude that there is likely nothing one person or one family can do to address a structural reality that oppresses millions of BIPOC. In many cases this is an instance of self-justifying indifference or a turn to apathy. In the Bible, the prophets often talked about those in privileged social locations or positions of power as having "hardened hearts" in the face of their suffering sisters and brothers. Pope Francis has talked about this theme regularly in his homilies, addresses, and writings, highlighting how this

---

[6.] Ijeoma Oluo, *So You Want to Talk about Race* (New York: Seal Press, 2019), 230.

tendency toward shutting down or apathy in the face of systemic injustice continues in various areas of our contemporary society. In his 2015 encyclical *Laudato Si'*, which was dedicated mostly to the large-scale ecological crises that all the inhabitants of the planet face today, the pope considered how such overwhelming challenges cause people to freeze up and do nothing because, as Oluo noted about racism, the problem can just seem too massive. Pope Francis wrote: "Sadly, there is widespread indifference to such suffering, which is even now taking place throughout our world. Our lack of response to these tragedies involving our brothers and sisters points to the loss of that sense of responsibility for our fellow men and women upon which all civil society is founded."[7]

Pope Francis challenges us all to avoid allowing ourselves to be overwhelmed by the understandable immensity of such structural injustices as racism and global climate change. Action is not only possible, but it is also necessary. The pope recognizes how racism is a persistent, systemic, and always present threat to human dignity and life, even when it is not so easily seen. In his 2020 encyclical *Fratelli Tutti*, he writes: "Instances of racism continue to shame us, for they show that our supposed social progress is not as real or definitive as we think." Later in the document he adds, "Racism is a virus that quickly mutates and, instead of disappearing, goes into hiding, and lurks in waiting."[8] And in the case of racial injustice, it is up to white people like us—who unwittingly benefit from social privileges

---

[7]. Francis, *Laudato Si'*, 2015, no. 25, http://www.vatican.va/content/francesco/en/encyclicals/documents/papa-francesco_20150524_enciclica-laudato-si.html.

[8]. Francis, *Fratelli Tutti*, 2020, nos. 20 and 97, http://www.vatican.va/content/francesco/en/encyclicals/documents/papa-francesco_20201003_enciclica-fratelli-tutti.html.

in our communities and who have not only the responsibility but also the power—to effect meaningful change toward racial justice. Our inaction, our apathy, and our indifference may not affect us very much on the personal level, but they do affect the lives of people of color.

Oluo offers some helpful suggestions that have been echoed elsewhere as small steps that white people can take to aid in creating real change in favor of racial justice in our local communities. These actions include voting locally with racial justice as a key issue by which you can evaluate candidates. Our local elected officials often have more power in our communities than the average citizen realizes. These officials set budgets, establish local laws and policies, determine the municipality's public agenda, and more. Another area to focus on is the local school system. However, this requires a note of caution (as does all white advocacy regarding racial justice), because often well-meaning white people who have been used to being in charge or leading can unintentionally make matters worse for people of color. The 2020 *New York Times* podcast series titled *Nice White Parents* offers an accessible and instructive look at exactly how such efforts can go awry and potentially cause additional harm.[9] It can be especially difficult for parents to think of what is best not only for their own children but for all children in the local community. Oluo says it well when advising white folks, especially white parents, who wish to make sure that racial justice is a school-district priority: "Let them know that an inclusive education that meets the needs of *all* students is a top priority for you, even if your child is not a child

---

[9]. See Chana Joffe-Walt, *Nice White Parents* (podcast), *New York Times/Serial Productions*, 2020, https://www.nytimes.com/2020/07/23/podcasts/nice-white-parents-serial.html.

of color."[10] When additional advocacy or intervention is needed, we white people must work in support of the agendas of parents of color, and not only in support of our own personal views or wishes. For white people like us, who are used to being in charge and getting our way, it can be a lesson in humility, but it is also an important aspect of sincere allyship that we learn to follow and not insist on leading or setting the agenda.

Just as it is important to work for racial justice in the family and at home by means of increasing your awareness of presumptions, language, and behaviors that are racist, so too it is important outside the home and in the broader local community. One simple yet important way to put your commitment to racial justice into practice as a white person in a systemically racist society is, as Oluo describes it, by bearing witness. She writes: "If you are a white person and you see a person of color being stopped by police, if you see a person of color being harassed in a store: bear witness and offer to help, when it is safe to do so. Sometimes just the watchful presence of another white person will make others stop and consider their actions more carefully."[11] Just as calling out one's relative for racist remarks or assumptions at the Thanksgiving dinner table can be frightening, bearing witness on behalf of our sisters and brothers of color in public is never easy. But the alternative—*doing nothing*—is a form of complicity and an exercise of white privilege that perpetuates racial injustice. White Catholics have a moral responsibility to bear witness to racial violence, bigotry, injustice, and harm.

Anti-racism activists also point out that white people can use their influence, power, and financial resources to assist in

---

[10]. Oluo, *So You Want to Talk about Race*, 231.
[11]. Oluo, *So You Want to Talk about Race*, 231.

the quest for greater equity and justice by choosing to support businesses and organizations that are owned by or that assist people of color. They can also boycott those institutions known for discriminatory practices or views.

There are other ways white people can contribute to racial justice that are not always so immediately apparent. For example, advocating for laws and employment policies that increase the local minimum wage is a good start. Because of systemic racism, BIPOC disproportionately work in low-paying employment sectors where even small improvements in pay can positively affect the quality of one's life. Another area of advocacy that white people ought to engage in centers on health-care quality and access. As we have seen earlier in this book, people of color disproportionately suffer from lower-quality health care or limited access to sufficient health care. This disparity follows from the kinds of work people of color are frequently limited to performing, which is often hourly and without benefits. White people can use their voice, power, influence, and presence to advocate with people of color for changes in access to health care and universal access to health insurance. If you find yourself in a position of authority, leadership, or management in a workplace, you have a unique opportunity to advocate in this way—advocacy is not limited to the ballot box alone. White people can likewise engage in advocacy for police reform in our local communities. We saw in chapter 4 how distorted and dangerous the criminal justice system is in our country. We must use our unearned privilege and social power to work for justice. Justice cannot be served locally until the structures and institutions designated to protect citizens are held to account for racial bias and discriminatory practices. Catholics can rightly call all of these examples "life issues" because they directly affect the lives, health, and safety of our sisters and brothers of color. Indifference or, worse, opposition to such advocacy and constructive critique only exacerbates racial injustice and contributes to what John Paul II called "the culture of death."[12]

Most importantly, at the local level it is important to remember that one does not go this path or do this work alone. Work for racial justice involves and affects all people, those oppressed by and those who benefit from the unfair systems, structures, and institutions in our communities. Seek connections with others who are likewise committed to working toward racial justice in your community. This can include reading groups, community-organizing partnerships, local "Black Lives Matter" chapters,[13] school groups, and other associations of women and men committed to working for racial justice in the local community. Many Catholic dioceses, although sadly not all, have offices and coordinators that promote racial justice and other social-justice issues. These offices and their staffs are good resources for white Catholics to begin engaging in order to get connected with faith-based organizing at the local level. If you live in a diocese where there is no clear outreach or resource center for Black Catholics and

---

12. John Paul II, *Evangelium Vitae*, 1995, no. 12, http://www.vatican.va/content/john-paul-ii/en/encyclicals/documents/hf_jp-ii_enc_25031995_evangelium-vitae.html.

13. It is important to note that "Black Lives Matter" is a nonhierarchical, nonsingular organization; it is a movement that emerged with the protest cry "Black Lives Matter" in 2013 in the wake of news about the acquittal of George Zimmerman, who was charged with shooting and killing the unarmed seventeen-year-old Trayvon Martin in Florida. Given the movement's decentralized nature, it is wrong to conflate the unifying and important message "Black Lives Matter" with any particular organization or website. However, there are many local groups of racial-justice advocates who identify with the slogan and form communities committed to justice and systemic change using that phrase.

other people of color, let your bishop know that you want to see the local Church embrace this important life issue and that you want to be a part of that movement. Likewise, at the parish level there is a broad range of responses from local Catholic communities that are very involved in the work of racial justice to those who are outright hostile to the idea. Be an agent for positive change, be a Catholic who puts their faith into action and volunteer to help organize and educate your fellow white Catholics; your parish is a good place to start. There are also opportunities at the parish and diocesan levels to partner with other faith communities who are in many ways far ahead of American Catholics in advocating for criminal justice reform, supporting the Black Lives Matter movement, and advancing other social-justice priorities. Catholics in the United States, especially white Catholics, have a lot to learn from our fellow Christians in other denominations, as well as our sisters and brothers of other religious traditions, about what it means to be people who put our faith convictions into meaningful action.

At the National Level

In this last section, I want to highlight just a few ways we as white Catholics can get involved at the national level, since racial injustice is not limited to individuals, families, or local communities, but is a widespread and deeply ingrained part of United States culture and history. Much of what has already been outlined in this closing chapter applies at all levels, but there are larger organizations, resources, and opportunities for collaboration and advocacy beyond our local contexts. For example, one of the most powerful activities a citizen can engage in is the duty to vote. As mentioned earlier about local-level voting, the issue of racial justice can serve as a criterion by which national representatives and other political candidates are evaluated. Catholics in general, and white Catholics in particular, have increasingly fallen into the temptation to be "single-issue voters." Despite the American bishops' efforts to help disabuse Catholics in the United States of this fallacy, it continues to be a problem during each election cycle.[14] I am not suggesting that Catholics replace one single issue with another, but instead I want to encourage all of us to remember that there is a consistent ethic of life that the Church promotes. This means that any assault on the dignity and value of the human person at any stage of life or in any particular demographic category is sinful and must be addressed. Systemic racism is one such form of widespread assault on the dignity and value of human persons in the United States, and therefore we must factor this into our evaluation of political candidates and the wide range of policies they propose. As white Catholics we might ask ourselves not only whether these proposed policies will affect *me personally* in a beneficial way but also how these policies might affect people of color in our communities and beyond.

There are numerous organizations that prioritize racial justice as their mission. Some of these include the Equal Justice Initiative, which was founded by the renowned activist and lawyer Bryan Stevenson and is committed to providing legal services for prisoners who may have been wrongly convicted of crimes; the NAACP, which was founded in 1909 to advocate on behalf of Black Americans in a number of capacities; the Southern Poverty Law Center (SPLC), which focuses its work on providing legal protection of civil rights and works against

---

[14.] The USCCB's quadrennial voting guide, "Forming Consciences for Faithful Citizenship," names numerous life issues that ought to be considered when evaluating political candidates and policies, including racism.

hate groups in the United States; and the National Council for Incarcerated and Formerly Incarcerated Women and Girls, which advocates on behalf of women and girls who have been imprisoned. If you are able to contribute to organizations such as these financially, that is one important means of support at the national level. However, learning about their respective missions and work, helping to spread the word, and perhaps volunteering as you are qualified and able are ways to advance the cause of racial justice in the United States too.

Pope Francis has regularly reminded Catholics that we are meant to be bridge-builders and people of dialogue, which should challenge white Catholics in particular to embrace partnering with other religious organizations and nonreligious organizations to advance the work of justice and peace in our world. Support for and partnering with organizations such as those named above does not necessarily mean that you fully endorse each aspect of their broad outreach or every dimension of their mission statements. Too many people excuse themselves from collaboration with other organizations because they cannot endorse every single aspect of an organization's agenda, but partnering with others in the work for justice or supporting a particular cause does not necessarily equal blanket endorsement of everything the partner supports (and vice versa). What it does mean is that you are committed to collaboration on the issue of racial justice and, as a white Catholic, that collaboration arises from the most fundamental principles of *your* particular religious convictions.

Finally, since the Catholic Church in the United States has significant influence in so many areas of social life, from health care to education to social services and more, it is important that we as members of the Catholic Church make an effort to let our Church leaders know how important the issue of racial justice is to us. As outlined in chapter 5, there is ample justification—from the Second Vatican Council to numerous papal statements—to encourage us to enculturate the call for racial justice within our distinctively American context. While the United States bishops have collectively published statements on the sin of racism and have issued calls for racial justice, the efforts have been less than efficacious and at times even counterproductive. Strong, direct, unequivocal leadership at the national level is needed, and we can each advocate for this from those entrusted with leadership in our faith community, especially the bishops in the United States. There is much more work that is needed, including at the national level in the Church, but that work will not advance unless all the baptized—but especially white Catholics—insist on it and contribute to the important pastoral and communal work needed in the quest for racial justice.

The Urgent Call of Now

The title of this concluding chapter is taken from a book written by Martin Luther King Jr. but published posthumously just a few months after his assassination in 1968.[15] In the very last paragraph of King's challenging book, which reflects on the intersecting injustices of racism, poverty, and violence, he offers a powerful exhortation on the need for immediate and decisive action by people of goodwill. He writes: "We are now faced with the fact that tomorrow is today. We are confronted with the fierce urgency of *now*. In this unfolding conundrum of life and history there is such a thing as being too late. Procrastination is still the thief of time. Life often leaves us standing bare,

---

15. King, *Where Do We Go from Here*.

naked, and dejected with a lost opportunity."[16] This call to action summarizes the immediacy, urgency, and direness of the problems before us. For too long too few of us white people have treated the sin of systemic racism with the urgent attention it deserves. Our privilege and sense of superiority, reinforced as they are by the dynamics of white supremacy discussed throughout this book, have frequently numbed us to the suffering of our sisters and brothers of color, especially our Black siblings. But King's words echo throughout the decades and ought to pierce our hearts. These are words of admonition for white people like me who might be inclined to recognize the problem of racism and white privilege, but put it off until tomorrow or later because I am preoccupied with other things that appear more important to me and my comfort now. As a Catholic, though, I find that the gospel of Jesus Christ grounds King's prophetic call and moves my conscience to repentance, lifts the veil from my eyes, and removes my hands from my ears so that I can feel, see, and hear the truth before me: that systemic racism and white privilege not only are real, but are always already operating to my advantage while also oppressing people of color.

This book was conceived as a guide for other white people, especially other white Catholics, to come to terms with the prophetic urgency that King names. It is by no means an exhaustive treatment of the deeply embedded and complex reality of injustice and privilege in our culture, society, and Church. But it is a beginning, and if you have made it this far, then it is a start. My hope and prayer is that those who have read the contents of this book, who have opened their hearts and

---

16. King, *Where Do We Go from Here*, 202.

minds to be challenged by discomfiting truths, might continue this important journey of ongoing conversion and work toward racial justice. The question "Where do we go from here?" that King once posed and that closes this book is not rhetorical, but invitatory. The way each of us answers this question will vary by the circumstances that shape our respective states of life. I cannot help but think of St. Francis of Assisi and the words he spoke shortly before his own untimely death. He said to those gathered around him, "I have done what is mine to do, may Christ teach you what is yours."[17] God certainly showed Martin Luther King Jr. and St. Francis what was theirs to do, and they responded to that call, which changed the world. God has also called each of us to do our part. The only questions now are whether or not we will take up that call and how we will put it into practice.

---

17. Bonaventure, *The Major Legend of Saint Francis*, 14.3, in *Francis of Assisi: Early Documents*, ed. Regis J. Armstrong, J. A. Wayne Hellmann, and William J. Short, 3 vols. (New York: New City Press, 1999–2001), 2:642. The English translation from the Latin is slighted adapted by the author here.

Acknowledgments

This book has been a work long in the making, but the writing has been concentrated and intense. As I note in the introduction, I have thought about, discussed, written, and lectured on racism and white privilege, and their relationship to Catholicism for the better part of the last decade as a theologian and a pastoral minister. But it wasn't until Eileen Ponder, my editor at Ave Maria Press, reached out to me in the summer of 2020 with a request that I considered finally writing this book. She deserves the credit for, as we theologians say, creating the condition of the possibility for this book. The nexus of such tremendous suffering on an unprecedented scale in the United States during 2020 with the consequences of the global coronavirus pandemic, the renewed national awareness of the persistence of systemic racism manifested in the form of police brutality, and the political polarization that had reached a new level in the midst of a contentious presidential election formed the perfect storm of urgency that inspired me finally to do what I have been meaning to do for so long. Thank you, Eileen, for your encouragement, invitation, and editorial insight.

I was also already in the middle of writing another book at the time I felt compelled to write this book, which meant that the earlier book in progress would have to take a temporary backseat to this more pressing project. When I spoke to my editor for that book, Hans Christoffersen at Liturgical Press, he responded with alacrity and understanding, allowing me to postpone that project by a year to complete this current book. Thank you to Hans and the great team at Liturgical Press for your patience.

Gratitude is owed to four exceptional people who graciously agreed to read parts or all of this manuscript as I was writing it. First, to my dear friends and colleagues Fr. Bryan Massingale and Dr. Jessica Coblentz: thank you for your time, insight, feedback, and suggestions. My intellectual indebtedness to Bryan is evident throughout this book, but what is not always apparent from the endnotes alone are the generosity, encouragement, and support his friendship over the years has provided me. Jess has been a generous and critical reader of many of my books-in-progress over the years, and I cannot thank her enough for her continued friendship and supportive collegiality. Next, I want to thank two of my former students at Catholic Theological Union, Fr. Matthew O'Donnell and Ms. Jennifer Reid, both of whom are amazing pastoral leaders for the Archdiocese of Chicago and do tremendous ministry at St. Columbanus Catholic Church on Chicago's South Side. Matt, who in addition to earning a doctor of ministry degree from CTU is also an alum of the Institute for Black Catholic Studies (IBCS) at Xavier University in New Orleans, brings a wealth of experience and provided insightful feedback on this project as a white Catholic priest pastoring a historically Black Catholic community. Jennifer, whose master's thesis I was honored to supervise, provided support and encouragement and caught *many* of my typos. The feedback from all four of these readers strengthened this book. Any weaknesses in the final result are entirely my own.

There are too many other family members, friends, theologians, ethicists, scholars, and activists who have taught me over the years for me to name here in a comprehensive manner.

Know of my appreciation and gratitude. I am especially indebted to my teachers, colleagues, and friends of color, those who have taught me in the classroom, who taught me by example, who taught me by their writing, and who taught me by their witness. I have learned so much, have been lovingly challenged, and have benefited from their encouragement, support, and patience. As a white man in the United States, there will never be an end to my need for ongoing conversion and continual education. This book is as much a reminder to me of the work I must continue to do and lessons I must continually learn and relearn as much as it is intended as a resource for others. It is my hope that others will indeed find this a useful resource and that white Catholics in particular may find it an encouraging and challenging impetus to embrace our shared faith more deeply and put that faith into meaningful action.